RIVERS
of the
WORLD

The Amazon

Titles in the Rivers of the World series include:

The Amazon
The Ganges
The Mississippi
The Nile
The Rhine

RIVERS
of the
WORLD

The Amazon

T 60404

James Barter

LUCENT BOOKS®

THOMSON

™

GALE

San Diego • Detroit • New York • San Francisco • Cleveland • New Haven, Conn. • Waterville, Maine • London • Munich

© 2003 by Lucent Books. Lucent Books is an imprint of The Gale Group, Inc., a division of Thomson Learning, Inc.

Lucent Books® and Thomson Learning™ are trademarks used herein under license.

For more information, contact
Lucent Books
27500 Drake Rd.
Farmington Hills, MI 48331-3535
Or you can visit our Internet site at http://www.gale.com

LIBRARY OF CONGRESS CATALOGING-IN-PUBLICATION DATA

Barter, James, 1946–
    The Amazon / by James Barter.
        p. cm. — (Rivers of the world)
Includes bibliographical references and index.
    ISBN 1-56006-934-1 (hardback : alk. paper)
    1. Amazon River—Juvenile literature. 2. Floods—Amazon River—Juvenile literature.
3. Watershed management—Amazon River—Juvenile literature. I. Title. II. Rivers of the world (Lucent Books)
    F2546 .B275 2003
    981'.1—dc21

2002001091

Printed in the United States of America

Contents

• • • • • • • • • • • • • •

FOREWORD   6

INTRODUCTION
   One River for Two Seasons   8

CHAPTER ONE
   An Ocean of Water   12

CHAPTER TWO
   The Early Amazon   32

CHAPTER THREE
   The Floods of Fortune   47

CHAPTER FOUR
   The Floods of Distress   65

CHAPTER FIVE
   Preserving the Treasures of the River   81

   Notes   97

   For Further Reading   100

   Works Consulted   101

   Index   105

   Picture Credits   111

   About the Author   112

Foreword

· · · · · · · · · · · · ·

Human history and rivers are inextricably intertwined. Of all the geologic wonders of nature, none has played a more central and continuous role in the history of civilization than rivers. Fanning out across every major landmass except the Antarctic, all great rivers wove an arterial network that played a pivotal role in the inception of early civilizations and in the evolution of today's modern nation-states.

More than ten thousand years ago, when nomadic tribes first began to settle into small, stable communities, they discovered the benefits of cultivating crops and domesticating animals. These incipient civilizations developed a dependence on continuous flows of water to nourish and sustain their communities and food supplies. As small agrarian towns began to dot the Asian and African continents, the importance of rivers escalated as sources of community drinking water, as places for washing clothes, for sewage removal, for food, and as means of transportation. One by one, great riparian civilizations evolved whose collective fame is revered today, including ancient Mesopotamia, between the Tigris and Euphrates Rivers; Egypt, along the Nile; India, along the Ganges and Indus Rivers; and China, along the Yangtze. Later, for the same reasons, early civilizations in the Americas gravitated to the major rivers of the New World such as the Amazon, Mississippi, and Colorado.

For thousands of years, these rivers admirably fulfilled their role in nature's cycle of birth, death, and renewal. The waters also supported the rise of nations and their expanding populations. As hundreds and then thousands of cities sprang up along major rivers, today's modern nations emerged and discovered modern uses for the rivers. With more mouths to feed than ever before, great irrigation canals supplied by river water fanned out across the landscape, transforming parched land into mile upon mile of fertile cropland. Engineers developed the mathematics needed to throw great concrete dams across rivers to control occasional flooding and to store trillions of gallons of water to irrigate crops during the hot summer months. When the great age of electricity arrived, engineers added to the demands placed on rivers by using their cascading water to drive huge hydroelectric turbines to light and heat homes and skyscrapers in urban settings. Rivers also played a major role in the development of modern factories as sources of water for processing a variety of commercial goods and as a convenient place to discharge various types of refuse.

For a time, civilizations and rivers functioned in harmony. Such a benign relationship, however, was not destined to last. At the end of the twentieth century, scientists confirmed the opinions of environmentalists: The viability of all major rivers of the world was threatened. Urban populations could no longer drink the fetid water, masses of fish were dying from chemical toxins, and microorganisms critical to the food chain were disappearing along with the fish species at the top of the chain. The great hydroelectric dams had altered the natural flow of rivers, blocking migratory fish routes. As the twenty-first century unfolds, all who have contributed to spoiling the rivers are now in agreement that immediate steps must be taken to heal the rivers if their partnership with civilization is to continue.

Each volume in the Lucent Rivers of the World series tells the unique and fascinating story of a great river and its people. The significance of rivers to civilizations is emphasized to highlight both their historical role and the present situation. Each volume illustrates the idiosyncrasies of one great river in terms of its physical attributes, the plants and animals that depend on it, its role in ancient and modern cultures, how it served the needs of the people, the misuse of the river, and steps now being taken to remedy its problems.

Introduction
• • • • • • • • • • • • • • • • • •

One River for Two Seasons

The Amazon is a single mighty river with two distinct personalities. For six months of the year, the Amazon carves its way through the majestic rain forests of South America carrying billions of gallons of water on its path to the Atlantic Ocean. During this season, the Amazon is like most other powerful rivers of the world as it flows toward the sea, following a well-defined route. Unlike most other great rivers, however, the Amazon turns into a very different river the other six months of the year when the floods arrive.

During the flood season, fed by monsoon rains and melted snow, the Amazon overpowers its banks, inundating the adjacent landscape for as far as twenty miles in either direction. During this season, the river quadruples in size as its waters spread across the bordering floodplain. The flooding can be so extreme in some areas that forests are submerged beneath as much as fifty feet of water for as long as several months.

At the height of the flood, the forest canopy that is home to a variety of exotic birds, lizards, and monkeys during the dry season becomes a watery home for fish and aquatic reptiles. Here, in the shelter of submerged tree trunks, branches, and leaves, aquatic animals breed and mature before migrating back to the main river channel along with the receding waters.

It is this annual cycle of flooding followed by receding waters that defines the lands along the Amazon River. Unlike swamp forests, which are permanently saturated, or temperate forests where rainfall can be scarce, floodplain forests depend on alternating wet and dry conditions. Limnologists, biologists who study freshwater ecosystems, note that the vast Amazon region, which consists of rivers, forests, lakes, and grasslands, is not one large ecosystem but, rather, a collection of dozens of smaller ones. Each ecosystem has unique characteristics but they all share two primary components: the Amazon River and its floodplain.

A cattle rancher gazes out the window at partially submerged corrals during the annual flooding of the Amazon River.

Villagers living along the Amazon depend on the river for fish and on the floodplain's trees for lumber to build boats and houses.

The scientific community has recently expressed concern about the well-being of the Amazon River and its floodplain. Since the early 1980s, research has focused on the upland Amazon rain forests, far from the river and floodplain. The disappearance of rain forests as bulldozers' blades carve highways and vast stretches of forest are consumed by fire has drawn headlines. The mighty Amazon River and its floodplain, however, suffer from the same depredations yet receive little media attention. According to noted limnologists Michael Goulding, Nigel Smith, and Dennis Mahar, the Amazon River floodplain is "the most endangered habitat in the Amazon Basin." [1]

Although the Amazon River and its floodplains constitute no more than 2 to 3 percent of the Amazon Basin, this relatively small area is of enormous importance to the region and its peoples. It is here that the residents of hundreds of villages depend on the fish that come to spawn each year, the floodplain trees that provide lumber for their homes and fruit for their tables, and a few simple crops for making their breads.

The environmental cost of such activities, however, has many scientists troubled. These experts believe that the exploitation of the region's resources, although it has improved the standard of living for many inhabitants, now poses long-term threats to the natives' way of life. Although the Amazon River continues to alternate between its seasonal flow and flood, it is showing signs of ill health, causing many groups around the world to come to the aid of this unique river and the peoples who depend on it.

1
· · · · · · · · · ·

An Ocean of Water

Satellites passing high above South America's Amazon River Basin transmit back vivid images of a lush verdant carpet interwoven with a complex system of rivers and streams that distinctly thread their way through the greenery. However, limnologists who descend onto the floor of this seemingly endless jungle report that the river is more accurately described not as distinct streams but as a flood or an ocean of water throughout the forest.

This description is appropriate, given the Amazon River's massive output. Second in length only to the Nile River in Africa, the Amazon nonetheless carries far more water than any river in the world. In a single hour, the Amazon discharges an average of about 170 billion gallons—sixty times the Nile's output. This outflow into the Atlantic accounts for a staggering 20 percent of all the freshwater that flows to all the oceans of the world.

The enormity of this ocean of water is the result of the unusually high number of tributaries—estimated to be as many as fifteen thousand—that make up the most extensive river system in the world. The area drained by the Amazon and its tributaries is almost beyond comprehension. Encompassing 2.3 million square miles of territory within seven different countries, the Amazon River Basin is three-quarters the size of the continental United States. As a result of the Amazon's annual flood, coupled with its vast network of tributaries, the river has often been called the Mediterranean Sea of South America.

The Amazon's incredible volume of water, especially during the annual flood that washes across millions of acres of adjacent lands, causes researchers to debate where the land ends and the river begins. Limnologists Goulding, Smith,

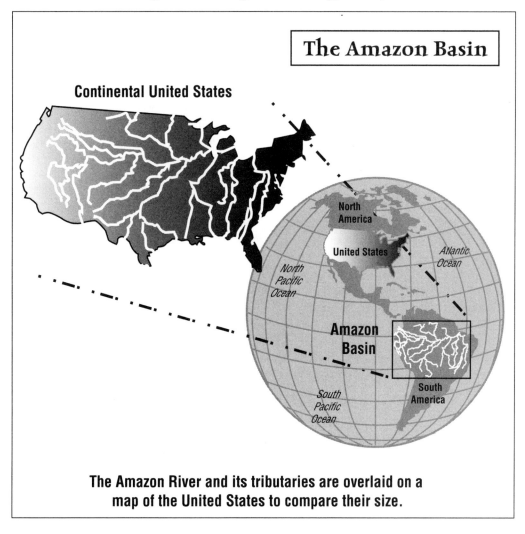

The Amazon River and its tributaries are overlaid on a map of the United States to compare their size.

The River and the Rain Forest

The Amazon River gives life to the world's largest tropical rain forest. According to biologists, without the scatter arteries of the Amazon River, this vast habitat, unrivaled in terms of biodiversity, could not exist.

During the annual floods, many regions in the Amazon rain forest receive rich nutrients delivered to the roots of their trees and plants. The floodwaters acquire their nutrient-rich composition near many of the Amazon's tributaries high in the Andes Mountains and from the Guiana Highlands. Every year, these mountainous areas release millions of tons of minerals and soils that help fertilize the thick lush growth of the forests. The rivers also deposit large quantities of organic-rich detritus that becomes food for trees as they decompose.

The rivers also provide the important function of ferrying and dispersing seeds. This process, a vital element of the rain forest's cycle of life, occurs in two ways. The most common is for the river to transport fallen seeds downriver, depositing them on fertile soil where they can germinate. The other occurs when fish eat seeds and excrete them, sometimes miles from where they were eaten. The pirarara catfish, for example, is known to feed on a regular diet of fruits and seeds that settle to the bottom of the river.

The rivers also function as a biological sewer carrying away forest debris, soils, and detritus and distributing it in other parts of the forest or washing it out to sea when the Amazon reaches the Atlantic Ocean. In this way, all forest matter is in a constant state of being recycled, which enhances the health of the entire rain forest habitat.

The rivers are so successful in helping to maintain the health of the rain forests that biologists estimate that one-tenth of all animal life and one-third of all plant life on the planet lives there. Early explorers dubbed the Amazon rain forest the "Green Hell" because of its dense forests and swampy land that made it virtually impenetrable. Even biologists have whimsically contended that the forests are so thick that an adventurous monkey could climb into the jungle canopy in the foothills of the Andes and swing through four thousand miles of continuous rain forest all the way to the Atlantic coast.

and Mahar acknowledge that uncertainty, saying, "The extended flooding season along the main river [the Amazon] and lower courses of its tributaries is the principal factor that makes the floodplain forests as much aquatic as terrestrial habitats."[2]

Hydrologists, scientists who study the properties and circulation of water, researching the Amazon and its floodplain report that this colossal flood of water is not one continuous river from its source in the Andes Mountains to its destination on the Atlantic coast. Rather, its flow consists of a complex tapestry of thousands of tributaries that weave and twist their way together to form larger rivers, which in turn combine with other tributaries to eventually create the Amazon River. In this regard, hydrologists describe the Amazon as a system of rivers—a river of rivers.

The Amazon's volume is so enormous in part because of the contours of the Amazon Basin. The basin is shaped like a teardrop that narrows and slopes toward the east. The basin is hemmed in on the west by the Andes Mountains and on the north and south by two long, sloping plateaus that funnel water toward the center. As water pours from the mountains and plateaus, the slight slope toward the east gradually carries the water downhill to the Atlantic.

Although most of this majestic river flows through Brazil, the great sprawl of water begins its journey on the eastern

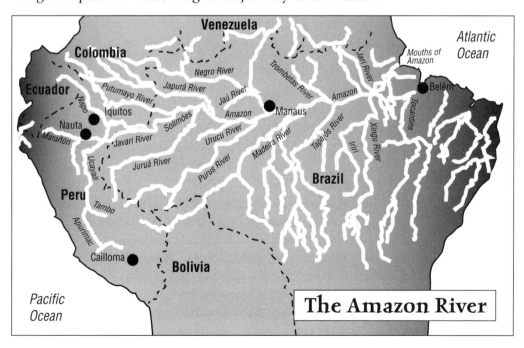

The Amazon River

slope of the snow-blanketed Andes Mountains that run parallel to the west coast of South America, just one hundred miles from the Pacific Ocean. Many of the thousands of streams that feed the Amazon are too small to even show up on maps, yet seventeen of these tributaries are more than one thousand miles long. By the time the Amazon concludes its journey at the Brazilian coastal city of Macapá, it has covered a distance of some forty-one hundred miles.

As the Amazon makes its way east through Brazil, it collects water from Peru, Colombia, and Ecuador to the west, Venezuela and Guyana to the north, and from Bolivia to the south. From its source high in the Andes to its outfall in the Atlantic, the Amazon constantly gains water as it moves east. The most significant contributions to the main river come from its source as well as its four principal tributaries, the Negro, Madeira, Tapajós, and Xingu. Each of these rivers is a major waterway in its own right, and each contributes the waters, minerals, and nutrients that ultimately make up the Amazon.

The Source of the Amazon

The headwaters of the Amazon are generally considered to be two rivers: the Ucayali and Marañón Rivers, which begin high in the Peruvian Andes and then drop down to skirt the eastern foothills of the Andes. Flowing south to north, the two rivers follow a parallel course until they meet near the city of Nauta, fifty miles south of the Peruvian provincial capital, Iquitos. Here, the two rivers are joined by the Napo River, forming the main Amazon River. The three then make a quick turn to the east on their course toward the Atlantic Ocean.

The Amazon headwaters capture the runoff from the twelve- to fourteen-thousand-foot Andean peaks when snow that has gathered all winter melts. These first trickles of the Amazon are called the *Huaraco* by local Indian tribes, who named them after the 17,000-foot Mount Huaraga. As the spring thaw begins, the melting snowpack provides an immense volume of freshwater that starts the Amazon's run to the sea. The river cascades from one series of waterfalls to the next until abruptly settling onto the floor of the Amazon Basin only a few hundred feet above sea level.

Rio Negro

Fifteen hundred miles east of Iquitos, the Rio Negro (Black River) joins the Amazon. The Negro is the most northern of the four major tributaries of the Amazon as well as its

Locating the Precise Source of the Amazon

In July 2000, a five-nation team on a National Geographic Society expedition in Peru determined the precise source of the Amazon River using advanced navigation technology. The success of their expedition was reported on the National Geographic website (www.nationalgeo graphic.com.

The team, led by Andrew Pietowski, used global positioning system (GPS) equipment linked to a satellite that was accurate to within fifteen feet. The team confirmed the ultimate source of the river as a small stream on an 18,363-foot-high mountain called Nevado Mismi in southern Peru. Andrew Johnston, of the Smithsonian Institution's National Air and Space Museum in Washington, D.C., who directed the GPS work, said, "The 'source' of the Amazon can be defined as the most distant point in the drainage basin from which surface water runs year-round, or the furthest point from which water could possibly flow to the Atlantic."

Mismi was identified as the source of the Amazon in an earlier National Geographic expedition, but recently, other streams had been in contention as the Amazon's ultimate source. Despite miserably cold weather below freezing, Pietowski was happy to report that "The trip's result is a highly reliable map of the Amazon's headwaters and an accurate determination of the river's source."

To accomplish this feat, Pietowski, and his team of twenty-two scientists representing the United States, Poland, Peru, Canada, and Spain, traveled by foot, Jeep, bicycle, and horseback to explore the five remote Andean rivers that combine to begin the Amazon River. The mapping effort found another stream to be slightly longer than that flowing from Mismi, but it was discounted as the source because it does not flow year-round in its upper reaches.

largest contributor, discharging an average of sixty-seven thousand cubic feet of water per second—four times the discharge of the Mississippi into the Gulf of Mexico. The Negro is a major river in its own right. Although considered a tributary, it is still the fourth largest river in the world. The Negro arises in the valleys of southern Venezuela and eastern Colombia, where it captures the runoff rains. Initially it flows south but then it turns in a southeasterly direction until its confluence with the Amazon at the city of Manaus, Brazil, fourteen hundred miles from its start. At this confluence, called the *encontro das águas* (Portuguese for "meeting of the waters"), the black waters of the Rio Negro flow parallel to the light brown waters of the main channel of the Amazon for miles; the combined rivers spread out to a width of twenty miles.

The light brown waters of the Amazon (left) run parallel to the darker waters of the Rio Negro (right).

The Rio Negro is so dark because it is saturated with millions of tons of decaying organic materials, known as detritus, washed along by the river. Most of the detritus contains high concentrations of humic acids or tannins common to

plants in the region. Unlike most other rivers, the Negro lacks the microorganisms that normally filter and clean the detritus, so the water remains almost black until it finally mingles with the waters of the Amazon itself. In spite of its color, the Rio Negro is home to a remarkable abundance of fish and other animals that depend on its waters.

Rio Madeira

One hundred miles east of Manaus, the Rio Madeira (Portuguese for "river of wood") joins the Amazon. The Madeira takes its name from the number of uprooted trees that once floated down its waters. This is the longest tributary of the Amazon, flowing northeast for more than two thousand miles before its confluence with the Amazon. The Rio Madeira's headwaters are on the boundary between Brazil and Bolivia, where more than ninety tributaries meet.

The mouth of the Rio Madeira is nearly two miles wide, and the river is navigable for large ships seven hundred miles upstream, until they reach a series of rapids. Because of the river's location, it receives some of the heaviest rainfall in the Amazon Basin, as much as 150 inches a year. During heavy rains, the river may rise up to fifteen feet, overflowing its banks and inundating nearby lands. The floodwaters deposit nutrient-rich sediments on the floodplain floor.

Rio Tapajós

Three hundred miles east of the confluence with the Rio Madeira, the Amazon is joined by the Rio Tapajós just north of the city of Santarém. The Tapajós is formed by the confluence of the Teles Pires and the Juruena Rivers, which arise in the Brazilian Highlands. The most southern of all Amazon tributaries, the Tapajós flows northeast to its confluence with the Amazon following a journey of eight hundred miles. The Tapajós accumulates much of its flow from an old geologic formation of rocks in the Brazilian Highlands, where sediment levels are unusually low; consequently, the water runs clear and blue.

For Brazil, this river is an important commercial waterway. Watercraft provide a transportation link between central and northern Brazil, and in spite of several rapids, the entire length of the Tapajós is navigable year-round.

Rio Xingu

The Rio Xingu is the last of the principal tributaries to join the Amazon. Flowing south to north, the river is formed by the union of three streams in the northern section of the plateau of Mato Grosso, in central Brazil. It joins the Amazon after a journey of about twelve hundred miles between the cities of Santarém and Macapá.

The Xingu is the most difficult of all the major tributaries to navigate. Following the confluence of the three streams that form it, the Xingu begins a long succession of rapids for four hundred miles. About one hundred miles from its mouth, the river makes a bend to the east and flows across a rocky barrier. Here, the river rushes down a gentle slope for three miles and takes a final drop over the Itamaraca waterfall.

When the Xingu meets the Amazon, it spreads out into an immense lake. Its waters then mingle with those of the Amazon through a labyrinth of natural canals that wind in countless directions through a wooded archipelago.

By the time all the major tributaries join the Amazon, the width of the river ranges from two miles to as many as fifty. Yet, at the river's mouth, the width expands even farther across a delta for three hundred miles. The depth of the thundering Amazon ranges from 50 to 160 feet, allowing large oceangoing freighters to travel for one thousand miles upriver to the port of Manaus year-round and twenty-five hundred miles to Iquitos, Peru, during the flood season. This is the farthest distance up the course of any river in the world that is accessible by large seagoing vessels.

The Interplay Between the Amazon and the Atlantic

When the Amazon reaches the Atlantic Ocean, the result is the world's most dramatic encounter between fresh and salt water. Marine hydrologists conclude that the eruption of

The Geology of the Amazon

The remarkable size of the Amazon network of rivers that unfolds, encompassing millions of square miles of South America, is the result of the low-lying basin through which the Amazon flows. Geologists explain that more than 150 million years ago, the Amazon River Basin was an arm of the ocean extending from the Atlantic to the Pacific, dividing South America in half. Since then, three geologic events have occurred to create the Amazon Basin.

The first occurred between 65 million and 138 million years ago when the Pacific tectonic plate began to slowly slide beneath the South American plate, creating a massive upheaval forming the Andes Mountain range. As the Andes gradually rose in height, they sealed off the ocean channel connecting the Pacific and Atlantic Oceans at the western end. Over millions of years, melting snow on the new Andes began flowing down the eastern side of the mountains, gradually filling in the ocean floor with sediment while pushing the ocean farther east.

The second geologic event occurred when a huge east-to-west upland region began to form along the northern border of the Amazon Basin, now called the Guiana Highlands, and along the southern border, now the Brazilian Highlands. These two massive plateaus sit at an elevation higher than the Amazon Basin, and as heavy rains fall on them, they act as a funnel, contributing to the melted snow flowing from the Andes. At this time, the Amazon Basin may have been the largest lake and swamp system that the earth has ever known.

The final geologic event contributing to the formation of the present-day Amazon Basin occurred about 1.6 million years ago when the sea level dropped by more than three hundred feet, providing the upper course of the Amazon River with enough slope to complete its run to the Atlantic. Michael Goulding, the author of many books on the Amazon River, measured the current slope of the river from the Peruvian border to the Atlantic and determined it to be a mere 180 feet over 1,500 miles. This gradual slope of an average ratio of about 1:69,000, meaning one foot of vertical drop for every thirteen miles of horizontal run, creates a virtually flat basin. Such a slight slope causes the waters of the Amazon to flow very slowly, which in turn causes its massive volume to fan out across the basin.

freshwater dramatically reduces the salinity of the ocean in an arc more that one thousand square miles around the mouth, causing some saltwater fish to vacate this zone. The Amazon's glut of water and sediment, estimated to be 3 million tons annually, is so voluminous that satellite photographs show the color of the Atlantic Ocean at this meeting point to be light brown for a distance of two hundred miles out to sea.

The estuary that forms where the Amazon enters the Atlantic is roughly 150 miles in width, but during the flood, that width doubles. Here, deposits of soil carried by the river have formed a maze of hundreds of islands that separate the river into branches. The mouth of the main stream is 50 miles wide. This branch, known as the Pará, is separated from a smaller branch by Marajó Island, which has an area of fourteen thousand square miles.

Just as the Amazon dilutes the Atlantic, so too the Atlantic invades the Amazon. During new and full moons, waves from the ocean called tidal bores have been known to sweep as much as six hundred miles upriver to the city of Óbidos. These tidal bores can be destructive, since they can travel at the rate of forty-five miles an hour, creating sixteen-foot saltwater swells that wash over the banks of the river. Local villagers fear these sudden invasions of the Atlantic. Tidal bores can pick up and carry large logs and even whole uprooted trees, sending them smashing into boats and buildings with enough force to destroy anything that sustains a direct hit. This massive inland flush of salt water creates an unusual aquatic environment suitable to both freshwater and saltwater fish. Amazon villagers living several hundred miles from the coast often report catching shark, tarpon, sawfish, swordfish, and porpoise, all of which are generally found only in the open ocean.

The Floodplain

As dramatic as the river itself can be and as rich as its waters are, the Amazon floodplain, locally called the *várzea,* is a unique gift of the river. Flooded half the year and moist much of the other six months, the *várzea* is unlike any other forest

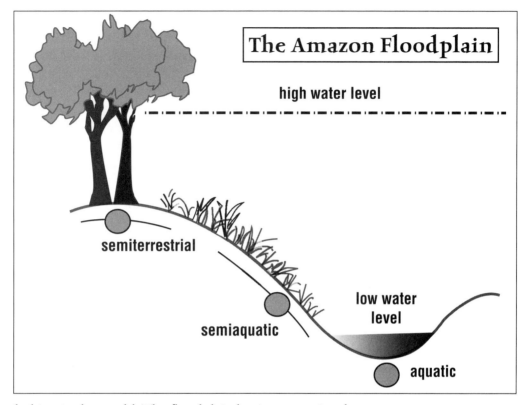

habitat in the world. The floodplain begins to receive the seasonal floods in late November or early December. Over the next few months, the floodplain is hit by a deluge of water that overwhelms plateaus and meadows, forcing animals and people to abandon their homes to seek higher ground.

As the waters inundate the land, many of the distinct features of the landscape become submerged. At the height of the flood season, the *várzea* becomes a water world where the trunks of trees disappear into dark depths that are home to large aquatic animals such as freshwater dolphins, more than a hundred species of fish, and the occasional Amazon manatee and caiman, a relative of the alligator.

The extent of flooding varies from year to year. Some years flooding can be extreme, while other years it might be minimal. In extreme years, the waters reach depths of fifty feet and the land remains flooded for most of the remainder of the year, preventing land animals from returning. In minimal years, much of the *várzea* is dry, with only a foot or two of water covering the low ground. In such years, migratory fish are prevented from finding safe spawning grounds. The volume of floodwaters is the result of two climatic conditions: rain and snowmelt. During much of the year, the Amazon Basin is hit by torrential rain. Some areas receive rain on a daily basis; others anticipate drenching monsoon rains during the wet winter season that can dump several inches an hour. Many isolated areas in the Amazon Basin receive between ten and thirteen feet of rain annually. Yet even some of the highest rainfall on the earth does not alone explain the predictable thirty- to fifty-foot surges in the Amazon's water level or the record rise in the city of Manaus at sixty feet above the riverbanks.

The other explanation for the annual flood lies in the Andean reservoir of snow and ice. Hydrologists explain that the seasonal snowmelt in the mountains creates a watery force twelve times more powerful than the Mississippi. Each second, an estimated 7 million cubic feet of water cascade from their slopes. When the snowmelt eventually combines with the heavy rainfall, the Amazon floods, swallowing up vast stretches of low-lying forests. As the floods advance, they leave no habitat untouched, engulfing areas many miles from the main channel of the river. By the time the flood crests, the forests are transformed into a spacious, slow-moving lake dotted with treetops and floating uprooted stumps.

As the floodwaters recede in the late summer, the *várzea* is replenished with nutrients—minerals and organic matter—brought by the flood. These nutrients sustain forest vegetation on which both animals and other plants depend for food and shelter.

Fauna

Within the 2.3 million square miles of the Amazon Basin is a wealth of animal life richer than any place on the earth. During the dry season, many exotic animal species flourish in the canopy of trees that stretch above the floodplain.

A Colorful River

The Amazon River changes colors along its length, with black and white waters sometimes flowing distinctly side by side and then merging many miles downstream. Four colors are recognized by hydrologists: White water flows from the mountains in the west from melting snow and ice; black water flows from the north along the Rio Negro that is darkened by detritus; blue water flows from the south filtered by the white sand of the central Brazilian Highlands; and brown water of the Amazon mainstream is colored by eroded silt and soil sediment.

The different colored waters that reflect the chemical composition of the rivers also have an effect on the abundance of wildlife living there. The white waters from the Andes contain a high content of minerals, including volcanic soils, that provide mineral-rich sediment for vegetation.

The blue-water rivers that drain from the south range from acid to almost alkaline, which, although nearly nutrient poor, provide an important mix when they meet the brown water of the Amazon that can be high in muddy sediment. As they come together, the blue waters dilute the concentration of mud, which benefits the fish stocks.

The black-water rivers carry detritus from the north and appear black because of the tannins of specific trees. These rivers lack the microorganisms to decompose the organic matter detritus, which mixes with the Amazon and eventually provides some of the nutrients needed by the plants and animals within the floodplain.

Without any one of these four waters, the wildlife in the Amazon River would be completely different than what exists today.

These include the world's smallest monkey, the pygmy marmoset, which lives in the floodplain forest but nowhere else. The tall trees are also home to macaws, harpy eagles, egrets, bald uacari monkeys, and dozens of species of lizards. During the flood season, however, the floodplain becomes home to hundreds of species of fish as well as fascinating creatures such as turtles, caimans, snakes, frogs, manatees, and the nearly sightless boto dolphins. These aquatic animals swim among the trunks and branches of trees, which just a few months earlier had been towering many feet above the forest floor.

The massive anaconda averages twenty feet long and can weigh up to 350 pounds.

Of particular interest because of its size and unusual habitats is the anaconda, *Eunectes murinus*. Of the more than one hundred species of snakes found in the Amazon Basin, the anaconda is the only one that inhabits the water exclusively. Although it is capable of moving to dry land, it rarely does so.

Lurking at water's edge, the anaconda preys on whatever animals come within its reach. Anacondas typically feed on large rodents, tapirs, capybaras, deer, peccaries, fish, turtles, birds, sheep, aquatic reptiles, and on rare occasions, people. Usually the snake strikes from beneath the water, biting its prey on the neck, constricting it with its coils until the animal suffocates, and then swallowing it whole, head first.

Anacondas grow to immense size, averaging twenty feet long, but lengths as much as twenty-five to twenty-seven feet have been documented. Claims of sightings of anacondas over thirty feet have also been recorded, but they are generally viewed with skepticism by herpetologists, who study reptiles and amphibians. The anaconda holds the weight record for snakes, with one specimen tipping the scales at 350 pounds.

Another reptile that makes its home in the Amazon Basin is the caiman, *Caiman crocodilus,* a relative of the alligator. The size of the caiman makes it a daunting predator that even the anaconda prefers to avoid. Caimans in the Amazon Basin grow to a maximum of about nine feet and four hundred pounds.

These reptiles typically spend the day warming in the sun on a sandy beach or rock. But caimans submerge themselves except for their eyes and nostrils as they await an unwary animal's approach. When one does approach, the caiman either uses its powerful tail to knock its victim down or erupts from the water to seize and drag its prey into the depths. Incapable of chewing its meal, the caiman spins its dead prey in the water until it rips apart, allowing the caiman to swallow whole sections. Caimans are capable of fasting for long periods of time, but when hungry they will eat almost anything that ventures to the river, including rodents, pigs, anaconda, birds, fish, river crabs, turtles, and frogs.

Perhaps the most unusual mammal of the Amazon River is the pink Amazon River dolphin, *Inia geoffrensis,* or "botos" as they are known in Brazil. Their pinkish color is

A caiman lurks in the river, waiting for unsuspecting prey.

due to a large number of blood capillaries close to the surface of their skin. No one knows the actual number of botos that live in the Amazon system, but along the Upper Amazon near Iquitos, Peru, researchers estimate their numbers to be about thirty-five to forty-five. In spite of its relative rarity, however, the boto is not considered endangered. Adults can reach nine feet long and weigh three hundred pounds. They tend to engage in solitary feeding strategies during the flood season when their favorite fish disperse into the floodplains. At other times, they congregate in small pods of four to six as they swim in the rivers to herd and trap schools of fish.

Flora

While zoologists marvel at the variety of animal life along the Amazon River, botanists find the variety of plant life to be even more remarkable. Botanists estimate that the Amazon Basin is home to an astounding eighty thousand known species of trees and fifty-five thousand species of flowering plants, half of which are endemic to the Amazon, meaning they are found nowhere else. No other habitat on earth supports a greater variety of vegetation than the Amazon. Botanists are also quick to point out that each time they explore new regions of the forest, they invariably discover new species.

Many of the plants found in the Amazon Basin are exclusively aquatic. Perhaps the most intriguing aquatic plant is the Amazon water lily, *Victoria amazonica*, the largest water lily in the world. This gargantuan plant grows saucer-shaped floating leaves that have measured seven feet in diameter and fragrant white flowers that are one foot across but blossom only two days a year.

These giant water lilies have one of the most bizarre reproduction cycles of any plant. On the first night that the flowers open, scarab beetles are drawn to their butterscotch-and-pineapple scent and crawl inside to feed on a sugary sap that collects at the base of the flower. Later that night, the flower closes, trapping the beetles inside. The following evening, the flower opens and releases the beetles, which are

The Piranha

Piranhas have an undeserved frightening reputation as small fish with razor-sharp teeth that regularly reduce animals wading through a river to nothing more than a skeleton in an instant of bloody carnage. Although many species of piranhas are carnivorous, many are herbivorous, and some omnivorous. However, even the carnivorous species are not the bloodthirsty fish portrayed in movies and fictionalized in books. Not all scientists who study piranhas agree on how dangerous they are to humans, but there is no proof that a person has ever been killed by a piranha. In fact, most piranha bites occur when a fisherman pulls a piranha out of the water and accidentally gets into its way as the fish flops around snapping in the boat.

Amazonians have been getting along with piranhas and making use of them for thousands of years. Piranha jaws are still used as cutting tools and their teeth as razors by some people in the Amazon Basin. Piranhas are also an important source of food. In Brazil, fishermen bait fishing lines tied between two poles or trees with shrimp and jiggle the poles. When the piranhas come to eat the shrimp, the fishermen lift them out of the water and club them on the head to avoid being bitten.

Piranhas are important fish in the freshwater ecosystem of the Amazon Basin and throughout most of South America. For example, piranhas can rarely catch and kill healthy fish, so they often eat the slower, weaker, or diseased fish. In this way, they keep the fish population strong and prevent fish epidemics from spreading. Because piranhas eat dead animals, they also dispose of flesh that would otherwise pollute the rivers.

Like the floodplains in which they live, piranhas are irreplaceable and unique. Scientists are just beginning to discover facts about the behavior and life cycle of piranhas, and the more they learn about them, the less people will fear these fascinating and mysterious fish.

Piranhas help keep the fish population strong by eating diseased or weak individuals.

covered with pollen. The hungry beetles then go looking for another bloom. As they settle down to eat, they deposit pollen on the pistil of the new flower and the cycle repeats itself. When the seeds mature, the pod decomposes, and the seeds are carried along by the Amazon's flood to start a new plant.

Of even greater significance, at least for the ecological balance of the river, is the water hyacinth, *Eichhornia crassipes,* which is found in abundance along the Amazon River. This plant is a free-floating perennial that grows about three feet in diameter and produces lush leaves and lavender flowers. As they float on the water's surface, with stems intertwining to form dense mats, water hyacinths provide homes for small fish and sheltered environments in which newly hatched fry can grow in safety.

Enormous water lilies grow several feet wide in the Amazon Basin.

The problem with hyacinths is that sometimes their floating mats become so large that they begin to have an adverse effect on the ecology of the rivers. In some parts of the Amazon, where the bends in the river are acute, these thick mats form habitats for disease-carrying mosquitoes as well as snail species that are hosts for schistosomiasis, among the world's worst parasitic diseases. Uncontrolled, water hyacinths can become so extensive that they damage water quality by blocking sunlight and oxygen and slowing the river's flow. The mats can block boat travel. Chunks of mat can also break free and clog pumps supplying water for drinking, irrigation systems, and even hydroelectric generators.

Most of the problems plants like the water hyacinth cause, however, are simply the result of human technology being ill adapted to the environment. The ancient inhabitants of the Amazon Basin had a comprehensive understanding of the river and its wildlife; they appreciated its significance in their lives and adopted their lives to the environment. Tribal peoples realized that they depended on the river as a source of water, food, and transportation. Its continuous flow and annual flood allowed their continued existence.

2

. . . .

The Early Amazon

No element of nature played a more significant role in determining the pattern of life for the earliest inhabitants of the Amazon River Basin than the river itself. Natives living in this enormous expanse of tropical forests owed their entire existence to the river, directly or indirectly, as the provider of their foods, medicines, transportation, and spiritual inspiration.

Archaeological evidence indicates that in ancient times tribes lived within a mile or two of the river's banks yet none lived right next to the river. Even though the ancient inhabitants of the basin knew that the Amazon River was the giver of life, they dared not underestimate its ability to inflict harm and even death. The massive flow of water, especially during the annual flood, was a force best avoided by humans. The ancient peoples therefore learned to live in the floodplains and fish in the shallows, rarely venturing out into midchannel.

Archaeological evidence of native settlements in what today are Brazil, Colombia, and Peru dates back at least eleven thousand years. Although the evidence is sparse, scientists believe that these early civilizations were sometimes large and complex. Large quantities of pottery and settlement mounds such as those found on Marajó Island, at the mouth of the Amazon, indicate that a prosperous society of more than 100,000 inhabitants flourished, more recently, in the first millennium A.D.

Anthropologists differ in their estimation of the number of people living in the Amazon Basin during ancient times, but most place the number somewhere between 5 and 7 million prior to the arrival of the first Europeans in the early sixteenth century. How these people lived varied according to location, but today anthropologists studying these ancient cultures place them in either of two general categories. The Tapuya predominated in the inland forests, grasslands, and plains, well away from the river; they lived by hunting, fishing, and gathering. The Tupí-Guaraní tribes, on the other hand, generally held sway in the tropical forests along the Atlantic coast and in the Amazon Basin closer to the river.

The Amazon River and its many tributaries defined the social lives of most tribes living in the region. Rivers functioned as boundary markers that separated one tribe's hunting and fishing grounds from another's. Rivers also served as the communication link between different tribes or widely dispersed settlements within the same tribe. The rivers were also the principal way that people oriented themselves to the landscape, gave directions to travelers, and described themselves. Most early settlements were located near some definable river characteristic such as a confluence, rapids, or a lagoon, and villages always incorporated some unique physical feature of the river into their name.

Of course, no quality of the river was more important to early Amazonians than the fish that lived in it. For many, fish were the primary source of protein and fishing was their primary occupation.

Fishing

Anthropologists and archaeologists working along the Amazon River have discovered considerable evidence that tribes dispersed throughout the 2.3 million square miles of the Amazon Basin depended on fish for a major part of their diet. Regardless of where they lived, whether along the main channel of the Amazon or a small tributary, many tribes referred to themselves as *Wai Mahi,* meaning the "fish people."

The changing characteristics of the river, its depth, swiftness, and flood stage, determined when and where fishing would yield the best results. Most fishermen, however, did not venture out into the middle of the river, especially during the flood season, because the currents could easily capsize their canoes. Most fished in the smaller tributaries where the water was relatively shallow and the current slow. Floodplains were also good places to fish since the water was calm and the fish would gather around submerged treetops to feed and to spawn.

Most tribes had a variety of fishing techniques, ranging from building simple dikes that trapped fish to the more exotic use of bows and arrows, spears, dip nets, and poisons tossed into the water. Fishing with hooks was a favorite technique because a line did not need to be constantly tended. The hook could be baited and the line tied to a tree and pulled in later in the day. The Indians knew what food the fish preferred depending on the location of the river, and they baited their hooks accordingly, using worms, insects, small fish, and even berries and nuts.

In areas of the Amazon where the water was clear and shallow, many tribes used bows and arrows to spear fish. The fishermen would walk along the banks or, if the water was no more than waist deep, wade in the river. Seasoned hunters were remarkably accurate with the bow and arrow and were able to land most of the fish they shot at.

Of all the early fishing techniques, the most efficient was poisoning the river water, although this approach was only practical during the dry season when rivers were relatively low and the poison could be used in a confined area. The men would build low dams of gravel, trapping the fish in a shallow temporary reservoir. Then they would go to the forest to harvest the roots of a leafy tropical plant of the species

lonchocarpus, locally known as *barbasco*, which contained toxic juices. The roots were beaten to release the poisonous juices and then the pulpy mass was washed in the water just upriver from the dam. As the poison filtered into the water, it would interfere with the action of the fish's gills, causing them to die of asphyxiation. As the fish floated to the surface, the village women paddled out in canoes and scooped the catch into their boats. Because they could be harmed from mild exposure to the poison, pregnant women were not allowed to take part in the capture. Instead, they helped clean the fish once the boats returned to shore.

Most of the fish were cut in strips, laid on racks, and then smoked for several days. Because of the heat and humidity, drying was not possible, and smoking the fish was the only way to preserve them for later eating. The fish that were not smoked would be placed in a huge pot and boiled.

Much as his ancestors did, this modern fisherman uses a bow and arrow to spear fish in the Amazon River.

They were shared among all tribal members in a fish-eating frenzy that might last as long as a week.

Early Aquaculture

Although the ancient peoples of the Amazon were expert fishermen, their success depended on fish being available. However, anthropologists are now finding new and intriguing evidence indicating that not all early fishing techniques centered on the chance findings of fish. A research team led by anthropology professor Clark L. Erickson of the University of Pennsylvania studied ancient mazes of earthworks located along portions of the Bolivian Amazon Basin. These features, which have been found on the floodplains near smaller rivers, include causeways of earth, canals for canoe traffic, raised fields for growing crops, circular pits for storing live fish, and fish traps called weirs. These various forms of earthworks have led Erickson to conclude that some early Amazon peo-

The ancient people of the Amazon used fish weirs like this one, which trap fish without impeding the flow of water.

ples transformed and shaped rivers to help them meet their need for fish.

Ancient fish weirs were fencelike structures made of wood, sticks, rocks, or basketry that extended across narrow streams and rivers. One or two small openings in the barrier allowed fish to pass through. Baskets or nets were then placed in the small openings to trap the fish. Although most fish weirs were simple temporary structures, those discovered by Erickson were part of a network of permanent earthen structures covering an area of more than two hundred square miles. Erickson explains, "Fish migrate to and spawn in the seasonally inundated savannas during the wet season. Many fish are trapped in water bodies as the floodwaters recede. The zigzag structures provided a means to manage and harvest these fish." [3]

In addition to the weirs themselves, small circular ponds were dug near the structures. It is believed that these artificial ponds were used to store live fish caught in the weirs, providing evidence for a very early aquaculture-based economy. This cultivation of fish through the use of weirs and ponds is a form of intensive aquaculture. As Erickson writes, "The fish weirs and ponds produced abundant, storable, and possibly sustainable yields of animal protein. Thus, they [the Indians] were able to sustain large dense populations in what many would consider a marginal environment." [4]

Hunting

Besides fishing, tribesmen also hunted for food. Hunting was very much a part of the lives of most Amazonian tribes, and many of the best hunting areas were those along the small rivers where many species of birds, reptiles, and mammals made their homes.

Hunting was an activity reserved for the men and was usually done alone except when pursuing unusually large and potentially dangerous animals such as the speckled caiman, the anaconda, and the large tapir. To catch and kill these large animals, tribal hunters used spears as well as

Capturing and Eating an Anaconda

Primitive tribes were known to capture and eat anacondas. Capturing a three- or four-hundred-pound snake in the water is a risky task. Documented evidence indicates that these large reptiles have eaten men as well as deer and wild pig that carelessly venture into the river. Whenever an unusually large anaconda was found, at least six men set to the task of capturing the muscular animal.

Traditional weapons such as spears and bows and arrows were ineffective against anacondas because of their quick movement and tubelike shape. Instead, hunters approached the snake with a more hands-on strategy. One man would grab the snake with both hands just behind the jaws while the others grabbed the bulk of the snake before it could wrap its coils around the man holding the head. If the strategy was successful, the snake was carried back to the village alive.

When the men and snake entered the village, there was always a festival because anaconda feasts were rare and because the snake was considered by many tribes as having spiritual significance. A painting found by anthropologists gives insight into how the snake was then killed. The picture depicts the snake hung by the neck from a high tree branch while a tribal member cut it open. The caption of the picture quoted in Alan Greerbrant's book *The Amazon: Past, Present, and Future* reads, "They wrap a rope around its neck, suspend it from a tree, and clamber up the snake like a mast until they reach the neck, then slit its throat with a knife and ease themselves down to the ground, cutting it open along the entire length of its body." Following the killing and skinning of the anaconda, the meat was boiled and shared by all the villagers, and the skin was discarded.

bows and arrows because they had to impale the large animals several times to inflict mortal wounds. An early drawing shows three men struggling to hold on to a noose around the neck of a large caiman while other hunters spear the struggling animal. Teamwork was particularly crucial in capturing the anaconda because the snakes often wound themselves around underwater branches, forcing the hunters to enter the water to forcibly unwind them. Once the hunters had loosened the snake's grip on the branch, they would drag the animal to shore to be killed.

The greatest hunting tool was the blowgun. The blowgun was a straight tube between six and twelve feet long made of a hollow reed. A dart, often a piece of bone an inch and a half long and sharpened at one end, was placed in the blowgun tube and propelled by a quick and forceful blast of air from the hunter's mouth. The hollow reeds were rarely perfectly straight and therefore did not shoot the darts in a straight line. Consequently, hunters learned to correct for slight curvatures. Despite this difficulty, skillful hunters were often remarkably accurate at a range up to eighty feet.

Because the dart was small, it was used primarily for small game such as birds and small monkeys that live in the high jungle canopy. Even for small game, though, the dart itself was too small to inflict a mortal wound, so it was coated with poisons made from a plantlike curare or with the poison extracted from the skin of the poison-dart frog that inhabited calm river inlets. Most poison-dart frogs were

Native Brazilians in traditional dress demonstrate the use of blowguns, which were used by ancient Amazonian hunters to shoot a dart at small animals.

roasted alive to derive and concentrate the poison, but one bright yellow species, *Phyllobates terribilis,* has such high toxicity that hunters merely rubbed the tips of their darts over its back. The effect of this venom on a human victim was recorded by the sixteenth-century Spanish explorer Gaspar de Carvajal, who explained what happened to a comrade struck by a poison dart:

> At the moment that it struck him he felt a great pain, and it was immediately evident that he was mortally wounded. . . . The right foot in which he had been wounded turned very black and the poison gradually made its way up his leg and when it mounted to his heart, he died, being in great pain. [5]

Nets and deadfalls were two other popular hunting methods. They were most often used to capture small animals such as the peccary, a type of wild pig, and the capybara, a rodent the size of a large dog. Both of these land mammals tended to feed and travel in herds. Hunters would set up nets or hastily dig a deadfall near where the animals grazed and then stampede the unsuspecting animals toward the trap they had laid.

Hunters often coated their darts with the poison from the skin of the dart frog to ensure a mortal wound.

Harvesting the Floodplain Jungle

In addition to meat from fish and other animals, early Amazon tribes ate a variety of grains, fruits, and vegetables. The torrential rain experienced in most regions of the Amazon Basin made it possible to grow a plethora of edible plants without having to implement a system of irrigation. Most native peoples were hunters and gatherers, meaning they would hunt animals and gather whatever wild grains, fruits, berries, and nuts they could find rather than plant crops.

Some tribes did practice rudimentary agriculture, however, and the soils of the floodplains were fertile. In such areas, people learned to reserve water from the floods in order to sustain crops through the brief dry periods. Those peoples who practiced agriculture would abandon their land as the floodwaters rolled over the banks of the rivers but would return once the river receded. While the floodwaters were still knee-deep, the farmer would use primitive tools to build low dikes to hold in some of the floodwater. According to anthropology professor Erickson, "The earthworks could have extended the period of inundation by capturing the first rains and holding floodwaters into the dry season." [6]

The primitive method of trapping water with low earthen dikes is known to anthropologists as basin irrigation, because building earthen dikes forms basins. Over a period of a month or so, the trapped water in the basins would eventually soak down many feet into the soil where the roots of plants could reach it.

Besides receiving the water itself, the floodplains would benefit from the nutrient-rich silt that the water carried. All the great rivers of the Amazon Basin with headwaters in the Andes are rich in sediment. These rivers erode the high, relatively young mountains in the process, picking up a huge sediment load. Some of the soil is volcanic, which is particularly high in nutrients.

Anthropologists have identified several small plots where basin irrigation took place in ancient times. They call these small plots "black soil" because their soil is very dark due to unusually high concentrations of nutrient-rich organic matter and minerals. Because the black soil plots are small, about one half-acre, it is assumed that the most common crop grown there was corn, which does not need large amounts of land to provide a bountiful harvest. However, there is some evidence that rubber trees may have been cultivated as well. Anthropologists believe that rubber was extracted by early tribes and that one of the earliest uses for rubber in the Amazon was as primitive syringes used to suck up liquids through a narrow rubber tube into a rubber bulb end.

Travel

In addition to being a vital source of water for early tribes, the Amazon River was key to their need for transportation. Travel on land within the Amazon jungles was virtually impossible because of the density of the forest. Although trails could be cut, they would be quickly reclaimed by the fast-growing trees, vines, and ferns. Moreover, anyone moving through the jungle had to run a gauntlet of poisonous snakes, which were numerous in the Amazon rain forest. Rather than risk their lives slashing their way through the dense vegetation, people preferred the relative safety of navigating small rivers.

Ancient Amazonians had to pay careful attention to the fluctuations of water levels when planning river journeys in their small canoes and rafts. When rivers, especially the many Amazon tributaries, were lowest, travel was both dangerous and physically demanding. Low water levels increased the probability of striking submerged rocks and tree stumps. When the water became extremely low, the paddlers were forced to drag their canoes and cargo across land until they came to a stretch of deeper water. On occasion, where low water was a regular occurrence during the dry season, villagers constructed earth dams to create stretches of deeper water so their boats could travel more easily.

The most common form of transportation was the dugout canoe. Traditionally, to construct the canoe, a man

and his sons went into the forest to find a tree with a thick trunk that would provide them with a twelve-foot canoe. After cutting the tree down, they began the process of roughing out the hull with hatchets until it was light enough to drag to the river. Once at the river, the work of hollowing out the log continued by burning the center wood until it was wide and deep enough to hold paddlers. Although the dugout canoes were heavy, they were sturdy.

An alternative to the dugout was the canoe made by one tribe, the Yanomami, using the bark of trees. The Yanomami first beat the tree with clubs to loosen the bark, which they would remove in a single piece. The ends were then folded and sealed in such a way to create watertight ends of the canoe. Sticks were then added from side to side to give the canoe rigidity and strength. These canoes were lighter than dugouts but much less durable. They rarely lasted for more than one or two trips before collapsing.

A man and a boy from the Matses tribe paddle a dugout canoe along the Javari River in the Amazon Basin. Such canoes, traditionally constructed from one hollowed log, have been used by Amazonians since ancient times.

Canoes worked relatively well for transporting a few passengers, but when cargo needed to be moved, the Amazonians would build rafts. Balsa logs seven or eight inches in diameter would be cut to equal lengths—about twenty feet. Using stones from a riverbank as hammers, workers spiked the logs together with wood pegs and then lashed them together with long strips of water-soaked bark. Balsa wood was extremely light and floated well. Each log could support an average of 110 pounds, so a number of logs together were capable of transporting heavy loads.

The River in Early Amazon Spiritual Life

The early Amazonian tribes were so dependent on the river for their sustenance and transportation that it became an important component in their spiritual life as well. Anthropologists believe that the Amazonian people were polytheists, meaning that they worshiped more than one god. Many of the rituals designed to honor their gods involved the river and animals inhabiting the rivers.

Various rites of passage are, for example, closely associated with the river. According to Jean Jackson, a professor of anthropology at the Massachusetts Institute of Technology specializing in Amazonian tribes, "Rivers are important to growth in a number of ways. One's humanness, one's self-image as a full-fledged being and a [member of the tribe], involves river ritual and symbolism. A newborn infant's first rites take place at the river's edge."[7] Later in life, young men would bathe before dawn in the Amazon and drink its water to give them strength to hunt and to fight against enemy tribes. Jackson also notes that a newly married couple's first sexual encounter would take place on the banks of the river, followed by a ritual bath in the Amazon's waters.

Anthropologists contend that the beliefs of Amazonian tribes involved spirits that were capable of mysteriously moving through the waters of the Amazon to assist people who were physically ill or in need of spiritual assistance. The

French anthropologist Philippe Descola, who lived with several tribes in the Amazon Basin in Peru and Ecuador, points to the beliefs of modern-day tribes and infers that their ancestors held similar beliefs. These spirits, Descola says, "move about at great speed beneath the waters of the rivers. . . . Each feels linked with his many unknown fellows by a river network that covers millions of square kilometers, through which he and his fellow spirit helpers can move about as if using a private telephone network."[8]

The river also figured prominently in the afterlife beliefs held by many early tribes. According to the traditional beliefs of the Tukanoan tribe living in an Amazon region bordering Colombia and Brazil, when a person died, he or she was carried to the afterlife in a boat made from anaconda skins. The afterlife, they believed, was a river called

The River in Tribal Storytelling

The importance of the Amazon River finds expression in many stories shared by early tribes in the Amazon Basin. Many of these stories express the importance of the river and river animals in the lives of the people living along the banks. One such story told to anthropologist Philippe Descola has been handed down for many generations by Amazonian natives and is retold in his book The Spears of Twilight: Life and Death in the Amazon Jungle.

Once upon a time the woman Sua lived on the shores of the river. One night she dreamed of a very handsome man and in the morning her heart ached with the desire to see him again. This man was Tsunki. Eventually he carried off the woman Sua and took her to the bottom of the river. There, it is said, he seated her on a caiman. The woman Sua was frightened as the caiman kept gnashing its teeth, so Tsunki gave her a stick with which to tap it on the nose every time it opened its jaws. Seeing that the caiman was becoming annoyed, Tsunki then seated the woman on a tortoise, where she felt much better. From there, she could watch everything at her leisure. She could see all the animals that lived with Tsunki, including the midnight blue anacondas.

Opeko Dia (the Milk River), which flows in the same west-east direction as the Amazon.

The relationship between the native peoples and the Amazon River was one of overwhelming respect. On the part of the Indians, it was a simple appreciation for the water that mysteriously sustained their way of life and a feeling of comfort that its abundant gifts would never cease. They never sought to analyze the river or to change it, because it provided them with everything they needed. Such a reverence and respect for the river was not, however, part of the beliefs of foreigners, who mostly saw only the commercial potential of the river and its surrounding land.

3

....

The Floods of Fortune

During the sixteenth century, Europe was in the midst of a grand period of discovery. Adventurers from nations such as England, Spain, and Portugal had found previously unknown lands across the Atlantic Ocean, and their rulers were sending men in great sailing ships to explore this New World and exploit its riches. To a far greater extent than these rulers and explorers realized, their fortunes were part of the bounty from the floods of the Amazon River.

The two most sought after natural resources were gold, which could be used to finance extravagant aristocratic lifestyles and costly wars, and exotic spices, which could improve the taste of bland and poor-quality foods. The early explorers who set out for the New World were often inspired by stories of the city of El Dorado, reputed to have been built of gold. More immediately, however, these same explorers hoped to earn gold by establishing trade routes to places where exotic spices could be found. In Europe, cloves, pepper, nutmeg, and cinnamon were rare and in great demand, so fortunes beckoned for those who could fill that demand.

The quest for trade routes yielded more than spices. Enormous stretches of seemingly unclaimed land were to be found. With high hopes for extending their empires and discovering new sources of wealth, the Spanish and Portuguese monarchs financed expeditions across the Atlantic to lay claim to the New World and its resources—whatever they might be.

Arrival of the Europeans

In January 1500, the Spanish explorer Vicente Yáñez Pinzón was sailing off the east coast of South America when

The Price of Spices

During the late Middle Ages, few commodities commanded higher prices than spices. Their use to improve the taste of meats, to prevent food spoilage, to make various medicines, to burn as incense, and even to embalm the dead made them indispensable for those who could afford them. Until relatively recently, the demand for spices, coupled with their scarcity, made them as sought after and as expensive as fine silks and jewelry.

Europeans were known to use spices as money. For example, a pound of ginger was worth the price of a sheep; a pound of mace would buy three sheep or half a cow; and pepper, always the greatest spice prize, was counted out peppercorn by peppercorn. Ten peppercorns in Spain would pay for a carriage ride of three hundred miles from Madrid to Lisbon, Portugal, or for a fine quality dagger. Slaves were reportedly sold for one cup of peppercorns each.

Ship merchants were always suspicious of the stevedores who loaded and unloaded spices along the wharves of Europe. Those on London docks, for example, had to have their pockets sewn up to make sure they did not steal any spices. On one occasion when a stevedore was caught stealing one sack of pepper by dropping it overboard into the Thames River, where an accomplice awaited it in a rowboat, both men were tried and put to death. And in 1609, when a record 116,000 pounds of cloves reached London in one ship, the owners weighed each individual bag before being unloaded and then a second time on the dock to ensure none disappeared.

In some places in Europe, spices were even used to pay ransoms. When a German tribe called the Visigoths threatened to invade Italy and destroy Rome, the invader negotiated a ransom payment of three thousand pounds of pepper, to be followed each year by an additional payment of three hundred pounds.

he made an extraordinary discovery. His sailors were test-
ing the depth of the water with a rope probe weighted at
one end. As they pulled the rope back in, they noticed that
the water spraying their faces was not salty. Wanting to
investigate this bizarre phenomenon, Pinzón ordered his
ship to be steered toward the shore he knew was just over
the horizon. In the process, he sailed about sixty miles up
what would one day be named the Amazon River. Other
explorers followed Pinzón, mapping various portions of the
river's mouth, but none ventured farther upstream than
Pinzón had.

Forty years later, the Spaniard Gonzalo Pizarro went to
South America in search of cinnamon forests. Pizarro start-
ed his explorations in the west, near what would later prove
to be the headwaters of the Amazon in Ecuador. He and
his men headed into the jungles on foot. Pizarro did not
anticipate the difficulties that lay ahead, and after eleven
months of hacking his way through the dense and disease-
infested jungle, he had advanced only two hundred miles.

Pizarro eventually found the cinnamon forests he was
looking for but realized that he would never be able to harvest the cinnamon and carry it back on horses because of
the impenetrable forests. Starving, sick, and dispirited,
Pizarro located a river, ordered the building of a small boat,
and appointed Francisco de Orellana to sail downriver and
then return within two weeks with food and help. Although
this seemed like a reasonable plan at the time, none of the
Spaniards knew how long a journey Orellana and his party
faced.

Orellana and the Amazon

Orellana departed on December 26, 1541, with a band of
men that included the Catholic priest Gaspar de Carvajal,
who as the only educated man among the party kept a journal of their expedition. (Carvajal's journal of their experi-
ences on the river would later lead to the settling of the
Amazon Basin by the Spanish and the Portuguese.)
Orellana ran into difficulties on the second day when his

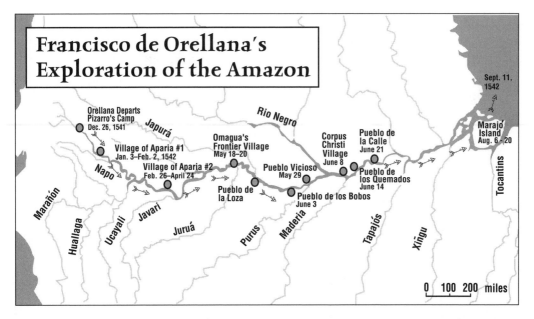

Francisco de Orellana's
Exploration of the Amazon

Sept. 11, 1542

Orellana Departs
Pizarro's Camp
Dec. 26, 1541

Japurá

Rio Negro

Marajó
Island
Aug. 6–20

Omagua's
Frontier Village
May 18–20

Corpus
Christi
Village
June 8

Pueblo de
la Calle
June 21

Village of Aparia #1
Jan. 3–Feb. 2, 1542

Napo

Village of Aparia #2
Feb. 26–April 24

Pueblo Vicioso
May 29

Pueblo de
los Quemados
June 14

Tocantins

Marañón

Pueblo de
la Loza

Pueblo de los Bobos
June 3

Huallaga

Ucayali

Javari

Juruá

Purus

Madeira

Tapajós

Xingu

0   100 200 miles

ship struck a log and sank. After repairing the ship, the explorers continued, but they quickly found themselves in the middle of a raging torrent of water that sucked them downstream with such force that they could not get to shore. Lost, hungry, and without hope of ever rejoining Pizarro, Carvajal reported in his diary, "We reached a state of privation so great that we were eating nothing but leather, belts, and soles of shoes cooked with certain herbs, with the result that so great was our weakness that we could not remain standing." [9]

Eventually, Orellana and his men were able to land at a village. The Indians there befriended and fed the explorers and gave them valuable information about the terrain. Orellana was astonished to learn that he was now seven hundred miles downriver from where he had left Pizarro. Recognizing that they could not turn back, all agreed to continue downriver in the hopes that the worst lay behind them. To their disappointment, however, the torrent gained intensity. Eventually, they realized that the river they were on, the Napo, was about to join an even mightier river. Carvajal reported,

It [the Amazon] did away with and completely mastered the other [Napo] river, and it seemed as if it swallowed it up within itself, because it came on with such fury and with so great an onrush that it was a thing of much awe and amazement to see such a jam of trees and dead timber as it brought along with it, such that it was enough to fill one with the greatest fear just to look at it, let alone to go through it. [10]

The Tragedy of Orellana

Not all explorers of the New World made great fortunes. After captivating the Spanish court with tales and exaggerations of his voyage down the Amazon, Francisco de Orellana received money to conquer the regions he had discovered. The money would allow him to explore and establish a town with three hundred infantrymen, one hundred horsemen, and the materials to construct two river-going ships. On May 11, 1545, Orellana departed from Spain with four ships.

Orellana sailed first for the Canary Islands, where he spent three months trying to resupply his ships. He then passed another two months at the Cape Verde Islands, by which time one ship had been lost, ninety-eight men had died of sickness, and fifty had deserted. Another ship was lost in the mid-Atlantic, carrying with it seventy-seven crew, eleven horses, and a boat to be used on the Amazon.

Orellana finally arrived off the Brazilian coast shortly before Christmas 1545

and proceeded up the Amazon delta. He constructed a river-going vessel, but by the time it was completed, fifty-seven men had died from hunger and the remaining sea-going vessel was driven ashore. The marooned men found refuge among friendly Indians on an island in the delta, while Orellana and a boat party set off to find food and locate the principal arm of the Amazon.

Upon returning to the shipwreck camp, they found it deserted; the men had constructed a second boat and set out to find Orellana. The second boat eventually gave up the search and made its way along the coast to the island of Margarita. Orellana and his boat crew set out again but were subsequently attacked by Indians, who killed seventeen men with poisoned arrows. Orellana himself died of either an acute illness or by drowning —historians are not certain which— in November 1546.

On June 3, 1542, Orellana and his party reached the confluence of the Rio Negro, as Carvajal explained:

> We saw the mouth of another great river on the left which emptied into the one which we were navigating and the water of which was black as ink. For this reason, we gave it the name, *Rio Negro,* which flowed so abundantly and with such violence that for more than twenty leagues [sixty-nine miles] it formed a streak down through the other water, the one not mixing with the other. [11]

On September 11, 1542, Orellana and his men reached the Atlantic just shy of ten months after parting company with Pizarro, who had meanwhile returned to Quito. Orellana and Carvajal eventually made their way back to Spain, but it was not a hero's welcome they received. Orellana was reviled because Pizarro had claimed he was a traitor for not returning with help. Carvajal found that his stories of the rivers, tribes, and jungles they had encountered were dismissed as elaborate fabrications.

The River of Riches

In spite of what many in Europe thought about Carvajal's story, some intrepid entrepreneurs were intrigued by his comments about the extent of the Amazon River and its lush growth. Of particular interest to these individuals were Carvajal's stories describing forests filled with exotic hardwood and spice trees, which they correctly concluded might provide them with handsome profits.

The entrepreneurs also correctly believed that the Amazon River might be a gift of another sort. They had heard of the difficulties experienced by Pizarro and his men attempting to hack their way through forest trails to harvest cinnamon, and were determined not to make the same mistake. Instead, they recognized that the river described by Carvajal might be able to function as a highway on which spices and hardwoods could be shipped back to Europe without the agony suffered by Pizarro.

Owners of ships that sailed the Atlantic were confident that their rugged freighters would be able to navigate the huge river safely without the difficulties encountered by Orellana on his small, hastily built boat. That confidence proved justified. By the end of the sixteenth century and the beginning of the seventeenth, as exotic spices such as cinnamon, vanilla, clove, and cacao began to find their way to European markets, the Spanish and Portuguese established colonies for the purpose of cashing in on the floodplain's bounty. The vastness of the Amazon Basin was perceived as an unlimited source of raw materials that would make fortunes for those willing to suffer the hardships involved in collecting them.

The Rubber Boom

The fortunes made during the eighteenth century from the trade in spices were enormous, but they paled in comparison to the profits to be made from another naturally occurring product, rubber. During the 1830s, Europeans began to discover the many uses for rubber, which was derived from the white sap found in certain tropical trees. One species of what came to be called the rubber tree, *Hevea brasiliensis,* was particularly plentiful in the Amazon floodplain, where the muddy waters provided the ideal mix of minerals and other nutrients. The annual flooding followed by the dry season provided a well-suited environment for this species of rubber tree.

Simple applications of rubber were known to early Amazon Indians, but it was not until Europeans began using it for waterproofing shoes and clothes that demand for rubber escalated in the mid–nineteenth century. Toward the end of the century, rubber was discovered to be an ideal material for bicycle tires; at the beginning of the twentieth century, its use widened to include automobile tires. As more applications for rubber were found, production in the Amazon Basin rose accordingly. In 1860, rubber exports in the Amazon Basin were about three thousand tons, but by 1911, exports had risen to forty-four thousand tons.

Tapping Rubber Trees

The process of removing rubber from trees, referred to as tapping, has changed little over the many centuries it has been practiced. The local Portuguese term for a tapper, a person who taps the trees, is *seringueiro*. In the wilds of the forest, each *seringueiro* maintains ownership of a distinct zone of about one hundred trees within which no other *seringueiro* may work.

Early in the morning, before the sun can warm and thicken the sap, each tree is tapped. Using a machete knife, the *seringueiro* makes an incision in the bark at a downward angle that extends halfway around the trunk. At the bottom of the cut that functions as a channel, he places a small pail to catch the rubber sap. Because the cuts are not deep and the tree trunks are very large, several cuts can be made each day, which will heal within a few weeks.

By midday, all of the small pails are collected, providing each *seringueiro* with about twelve pounds of rubber. He then begins the process of curing the rubber by building a fire, then dipping a wooden paddle in the thick liquid rubber, and slowly spinning it over the fire until the rubber forms into a thick mass. More and more liquid rubber is added to the paddle until the *seringueiro* has a ball, called a *pele*, weighing about seventy or eighty pounds.

After many months of curing, when the heavy rains arrive and the *seringueiro* has thirty or forty *peles,* he ties them together and floats them down a river to a trading village. Here, a buyer splits each *pele* open, grades it for quality, and then pays the *seringueiro* the market rate for his product.

A seringueiro *cuts a groove into a tree to tap rubber.*

During the height of rubber production, several hundred thousand Amazonians were employed as rubber tappers, the people who extracted the sap from the trees. As the rubber trade flourished, cities in the Amazon Basin began to prosper. The port city of Manaus, for example, grew from a rustic village of five thousand residents in 1870 to a cosmopolitan city of fifty thousand by 1910. Its modern amenities included a magnificent opera house, electricity, clean water, and mansions for wealthy rubber plantation owners. Manaus was compared to New York as a cultural mecca, and the wealthy could enjoy extravagances such as imported French champagne and perfume.

By the 1930s, however, prosperity began to fade. Growing rubber production in other parts of the world depressed rubber prices. By the 1950s, prices dropped even further as synthetic materials replaced natural rubber in many applications and the demand for natural rubber dropped sharply. The rubber crash left hundreds of thousands of tappers and their families economically distressed.

This nineteenth-century engraving depicts natives tapping rubber trees during the Amazonian rubber boom.

The Gold Rush

For many Amazonians, disaster was averted when, during the late 1960s and early '70s, gold was discovered throughout the Amazon Basin. At that time, the world price of gold was as high as $700 an ounce, an incentive for hundreds of thousands of poor Amazonians to try their luck as gold prospectors, locally known as *garimpeiros*.

One of the many productive parts of the Amazon Basin for the *garimpeiros* was the Amazon River and its many tributaries, specifically between the cities of Manaus and

Santarém as well as the entire length of the Madeira River. The Amazon River became the single largest source for gold in the Amazon Basin primarily because this precious metal is commonly found in alluvial deposits such as sand, gravel, and silt. As the river flows east, draining water from the Andes Mountains and numerous plateaus, it sweeps up millions of tons of mineral-rich sediment containing high concentrations of gold.

The alluvial deposits of gold were not only rich but easily tapped. *Garimpeiros* needed only the simplest mining tool, a pan, in order to begin prospecting. The *garimpeiro* filled this shallow round pan with sand or gravel, held it under a gentle stream of water, and swirled it in a circular motion. The lighter particles of gravel would gradually be washed over the rim while any bits of gold, because they are heavier, would be left in the pan.

Once it became clear how rich the alluvial deposits were, successful *garimpeiros* purchased machines to increase the volume of river sand that could be mined. Special elevator dredges were imported to scoop up the material from the river bottom and empty it into screens. The material was then rotated to separate the gold from the other particles. Other *garimpeiros* tried other techniques. One miner explained his method for working parts of the river that conventional machinery could not exploit: "I'm working the rivers with portable suction pumps and diving gear. These waters have never been touched commercially."[12]

By the 1980s, gold had become the leading export from the Amazon Basin, with production worth between $2 and $3 billion annually, the majority of which was mined in the river. Significantly, the gold kept coming. Because of the size of the Amazon and its constant flood of minerals coming out of the mountains, gold continued to appear in the rivers of the Amazon Basin.

As is the case with any mining venture, a small number of miners struck it rich while the majority worked hard for little profit. Many would-be miners who had traveled a long way and earned little looked for some other business venture along the river rather than return home empty-handed.

Logging Hardwood Forests

Along the river where miners panned for gold were impressive stands of hardwood forests. Although trees did not have the magical lure of gold, their value had been increasing and they were more easily found than gold. In addition, during much of the second half of the twentieth century, the demand for exotic hardwoods rose as nations in Europe, Asia, and North America prospered.

Logging the hardwood forests within the Amazon River floodplain created the third great flood of wealth along the river. Those harvesting hardwoods and the middlemen who milled, shipped, and sold the lumber both prospered. Amazon trees such as teak, mahogany, chestnut, walnut, rosewood, and ebony were prized for their extraordinary hardness and their beauty. Hardwoods from the Amazon

Brazilian miners extract gold from the Amazon riverbank in 1989.

Hardwoods from the Amazon were valued for their beauty and durability, but they were being harvested faster than they could replenish themselves.

were used for strong floors and to make furniture to adorn homes and offices. Builders of luxury boats used these hardwoods because they resist the rotting effects of salt water better than any other natural material.

Hardwoods grow throughout the Amazon Basin, but loggers found that thanks to ideal growing conditions they were plentiful and large within the floodplain. The floodwaters deposit a layer of nutrient-rich soil that washes across and fertilizes the trees. This annual renewal of nutrients does not occur in the upland rain forests, where the rainwater simply drains away. In addition, the floodplain receives more sunlight overall that stimulates their growth. The density of trees in the upland rain forests is so great that few hardwood trees receive adequate sunlight to mature fully.

Each year during the dry season, the loggers would return to the floodplains to harvest more trees. Felled trees would be stacked awaiting the next flood, when they would be lashed together to form rafts that were floated downriver to sawmills. Upon their arrival at the sawmills, logs were sorted by type, quality, and weight. They would then be cut into raw lumber and shipped to consumers around the world.

South American economists knew that hardwoods were being harvested faster than they could regrow, so they began to search for other sources of income for the people of the Amazon Basin. The idea was to improve local economies by diversifying. Cattle ranching appeared to be a natural alternative to logging as a way for the people to make a living.

Ranching

By the 1980s, large meadows had begun to take the place of fallen hardwood forests. Landowners took the advice of the economists and cleared away remaining trees and imported cattle, water buffalo, and goats. At the time, ranching looked like an excellent use for the cleared land.

A rancher herds his cattle in Rondonia, Brazil, on previously forested land.

In addition to the income they received from selling meat, local peoples would derive nutritional benefits from the milk and other dairy products the animals would produce. Indeed, despite the inconvenience of having to move livestock to higher ground during the flood season, ranching did give a boost to the economy of the region.

Ranching proved profitable to the ranchers. During the dry season, cattle and goats require very little care as they graze throughout the floodplain meadows and low shrubs. Even the annual flood was less of a problem than it might at first have appeared. Ranchers with fewer animals would construct floating pens called *marombas*, which are large rafts safely anchored to prevent them from floating away. They would also cut grass and ferry it out to the pens. Large ranchers, on the other hand, had to herd their animals to high ground. However, cattle ranchers could return their stock to the pastures before the floodwaters were completely gone, because cattle are capable of wading into water as much as five feet deep to eat many of the water plants that flourish during the flood.

Fisheries

While some Amazonians were beginning to learn how to raise livestock, others were earning a living by fishing, just as their ancestors had. Fishing on the Amazon River, which was once mainly a subsistence activity, changed significantly around 1960 to become a major source of income in the region. The local tribesmen who once paddled small canoes along the calm waters of small tributaries and floodplains began to find themselves competing with much larger commercial boats from Brazilian port cities such as Manaus, Santarém, and Macapá. Instead of individual fishermen using the traditional small nets and fishing poles, operators of these large boats would string out miles of gill nets capable of catching many tons of fish each day.

Fishing was profitable on the Amazon River and its floodplain thanks to an extraordinary diversity of salable fish. More than fifty commercially valuable species are found dur-

The Amazon River is the home to a diverse number of fish including the pirarucu (pictured).

ing the flood season. When migratory species that spend much of their lives in the main rivers are added, the number more than triples. High waters during the flood season allow large commercial fishing boats and fishermen in small boats to pursue the many fish that seek the protection of the submerged forests to spawn. During the dry season, however, only the large commercial boats can operate, since the swift currents of the main rivers destroy smaller craft.

It is generally in the open rivers during the dry season that the largest tonnage of commercial fish is taken using large gill nets and long lines. The most important commercial fish along the Amazon River is the tambaqui, a fish from the piranha family that typically grows to between three and four feet and weighs up to sixty pounds. The next most commonly caught fish is the piramutaba catfish. During the peak season, exports of this catfish were worth as much as $13 million. Second in export is the dourada, a type of catfish that grows to five feet and weighs up to fifty pounds.

In addition to these major fish are dozens of species of common croakers, rockfish, mullet, and the largest of the Amazon fish called the pirarucu, a long, black flat fish, which can grow to more than ten feet in length and weigh three hundred pounds. Besides the fish, boats operating close to the mouth of the Amazon River catch crab and shrimp carried upriver from the ocean. These crustaceans are local favorites as well as exports.

As a result of all of the various types of fishing, fish represent the most important source of protein in the Amazon Basin. In addition to their nutritional importance, they are also of enormous economic importance. Fishing employs more people than any other commercial activity in the Amazon Basin; the value of annual exports of fish has recently reached the $1 billion mark.

Electricity produced by dams along the Amazon tributaries, such as the Samuel dam (pictured), has provided great economic benefits to the residents of the Amazon Basin.

Hydroelectric Dams

The commercial value of the Amazon's waters go beyond the fish and other products that can be harvested. In 1974, Brazil—along with many other nations—suffered from a shortage of oil as major suppliers cut production drastical-

ly in order to raise prices. Because Brazil was a major importer of oil that was used primarily to fuel power plants, the nation's leaders looked to the Amazon River as a solution to their electricity needs.

Beginning in the early 1980s, Brazil initiated an energy policy focused on producing hydroelectricity by constructing dams on some of the Amazon River tributaries. The Amazon River itself was determined to be much too large and lacking sufficient slope to provide electricity, but several of its tributaries proved to be excellent candidates for damming. The three best geographical locations that provided steep slopes and the mountainous terrain preferred for hydroelectric dams were to the west, along the Andes and in both the Guiana Highlands and the Brazilian Highlands.

The two largest dams within the Amazon River system sit astride the Itaipu and Tucuruí Rivers, both of which drain water from the Brazilian Highlands. The Itaipu is capable of generating 12,600 megawatts of electricity, and the Tucuruí, 6,500 megawatts. This output ranks these dams as the two most productive hydroelectric generators in the world. In addition to these two dams, several smaller ones add to the tremendous electrical output that makes Brazil the world's fourth largest producer of hydroelectricity.

The economic benefit of hydroelectric power from the Amazon River Basin is remarkable. All of the large cities within the Amazon Basin now enjoy an uninterrupted supply of electricity for both commercial and domestic use. Even remote villages are beginning to enjoy the benefits of electricity as power lines are strung through the dense jungles. These dams are also saving all countries in the Amazon Basin billions of dollars that they once paid to purchase oil and coal to generate electricity. Even environmentalists applaud the additional benefit of reducing the pollutants that once spewed into the air when coal and oil were burned to turn electrical generators.

Despite the short-term benefits that exploiting the Amazon has afforded the people of the Amazon Basin, environmentalists and biologists are not happy with how the great Amazon

River has been used commercially. Scientists concerned with the health of the river fear that gold mining, logging, ranching, and damming will create long-term problems. As the twentieth century ended and the twenty-first began, there was increasing evidence that the world's most robust river is suffering from being overexploited.

4

....

The Floods of Distress

By the 1990s, the exploitation of the Amazon River's natural resources, which had once appeared to be responsible, was revealed to be environmentally destructive. As scientists began closely examining the river, they discovered that the water quality had markedly declined and that its vast abundance of plant and animal life was disappearing at a rate much faster than anticipated. Three biologists who have spent their professional lives studying the Amazon River noted in 1995,

> Floodplain settlement, farming, ranching, gold mining, and logging have already had a major and, in some cases devastating, effect on the ecology of much of the Amazon River. The Amazon River floodplain has undergone more environmental change in the last two or three decades than in all of previous human history. [13]

Analysis of the Amazon River and its floodplain reveals that commercial ventures, which were responsible for bringing modest prosperity to villages and towns along the river, were also responsible for most of the environmental devastation. In a matter of four decades, the river that had once provided a commercial flood of fortune had suddenly begun providing a flood of environmental distress.

Deforestation

Scientists consider the forests of the Amazon floodplain to be one of the best barometers for gauging the general health of the ecosystem. The reason for this is that the forests provide homes and sustenance for nearly all animals that inhabit them. During the 1980s, after many of the hardwoods had already been removed, evidence for the declining health of the Amazon River and its floodplain began to emerge.

Before the advent of large-scale logging, the annual floods would uproot old or sick trees, which the receding waters would deposit along the riverbanks. This deadwood would be gathered and milled into lumber or simply used directly to build rudimentary sheds or other structures. Collection of this wood had little effect on the forest, since the loss of old and sick trees was always balanced by the growth of new ones.

Once commercial logging commenced, however, tall stands of timber quickly disappeared. According to Professors Goulding, Smith, and Mahar, "In the 1970s huge timber rafts derived from floodplain trees were common spectacles on Amazonian rivers. By about 1980, however, most of the floodplain of the Amazon River had been logged, at least for the precious species." [14] Because of the prosperity that producing hardwood lumber brought to residents of the Amazon River, it did not occur to anyone to question the consequences of large-scale logging.

The animals that suffered most from the destruction of hardwood stands were the fish, which spawned among the branches of submerged trees during the flood season. Deprived of shelter, fish eggs and newly hatched fry experienced high mortality rates. Even for the fry that survived the first few weeks, fewer grew to adulthood because of their inability to locate ample cover as the number of mature trees diminished.

All fish, young and old, found less food. Many herbivorous species depend on the nuts, seeds, and fruit that fall to the water. Carnivorous species, meanwhile, depend on insects and spiders that make their homes among the branches. Without the trees that make these vital foods available, the young were dying from starvation or by being eaten by adults that could not locate enough other forms of food.

Other vegetation that provided cover for fish during the flood season also was destroyed in the process of harvesting

A man poses with his chainsaw in a Brazilian jungle that has been clear-cut for lumber.

Bulldozing roads through the Amazon floodplain has destroyed vegetation, resulting in fewer safe spawning areas and less food and cover for fish during the flood season.

trees. Logging companies bulldozed roads through the floodplain to provide access to the big trees for their heavy machinery. As trucks and hydraulic machines that grip and uproot trees ground across the floodplain during the dry season, they crushed all low-growing vegetation. The result was fewer safe spawning areas and less food and cover for fish during the flood season.

Scientists studying the deforestation of the river floodplain estimate the total floodplain area to be between 2 and 3 percent of the entire Amazon Basin. This is still an extremely significant area, however, because it represents nearly 100 percent of the spawning grounds for fish in the region.

Building Ranches

The way the deforested floodplain was utilized only made the environmental destruction worse. Governments of many countries within the Amazon Basin saw the newly stripped land as an opportunity for short-term gains. Rather than replant the floodplain with young hardwood trees that would provide lumber and would restore the dwindling fish stocks for future generations, they opted instead to sell the land to large-scale commercial ranchers.

To prepare the land for livestock, the ranchers removed the remaining tree stumps and any trees the loggers had left standing by setting them on fire. This method for clearing the land was cheap, but unfortunately, the burning destroyed more than the remaining trees and stumps. As fires swept across the land, many animals incapable of escaping were also destroyed.

Moreover, the fires proved hard to control. In 1989, for example, a fire was set in the Brazilian state of Para to clear a few hundred acres of land. The fire, however, burned out of control for several days, and by the time it was put out, 247,000 acres of selectively logged forest had been destroyed. Jim LaFleur, an agricultural consultant with thirteen years of experience working in the Amazon Basin, witnessed the fire from the air and reported, "When I [flew] over the state [Para], it was shocking. It was like watching a sheet of paper burn from the inside out." [15]

A farmworker sets an area of rain forest ablaze in order to clear land for farming and ranching.

The damage caused by the fires was only made worse by the subsequent action of ranchers. As soon as the brush and other natural growth began to creep back toward pastureland, ranchers sprayed herbicides on the plants to check their advance. Thousands of gallons of various types of herbicides, as well as gasoline, were sprayed from planes and trucks. Then, when the annual floods returned, residues of the herbicides entered the floodwaters, where fish ingested the poison intended for plants.

Further devastation accompanied the arrival of the construction crews. Trucks loaded with all the materials needed to construct ranches, barns, milking sheds, bunkhouses, and fences arrived. Roads were cut and leveled, thousand-gallon gas tanks were installed, and service stations for truck maintenance were set up. Electrical generators were trucked in and power lines were strung from one ranch building to the next. Long before the first large herds of livestock arrived, large portions of the delicate floodplain had been obliterated.

Invading Livestock

As large herds of livestock began arriving on the newly cleared pastureland, a second wave of problems beset the floodplain. The ground itself, flooded half the year and semimoist much of the rest, is well suited for small animals that move about without crushing the delicate soil and vegetation, not large hoofed animals with voracious appetites.

Cattle, goats, and water buffalo have insatiable appetites, and when herds graze along the floodplains, they have the same effect as a giant lawn mower. Especially damaging to the ecology of the floodplain are the water buffalo. Weighing upwards of a ton and standing six feet at the shoulder, water buffalo consume enormous quantities of vegetation daily to survive. The worst damage they inflict occurs during the end of the annual flood when the waters are receding. At this time of year, they are capable of wading and sometimes swimming out to the floating meadows to graze. Because the floating meadows are not anchored to the river bottom, dozens of these animals smash their way through the meadows, completely shredding them while they graze. Floating meadows are important assets to the ecology of the floodplains because they provide safety and sustenance for newly hatched fish as well as a variety of insects and other small animals.

Many delicate plants also suffer from the trampling of sharp hooves. The soils of the floodplain are unique because of both their high organic content and their high

Large herds of live-stock, such as cattle, destroy the delicate floodplain.

moisture content following the floods. But livestock, espe-cially heavy cattle and water buffalo, trample and kill del-icate young roots of grasses and other plants. Once large tracts of new grasses are killed and the drying soil is tram-pled, the bare dirt is further compacted. Over time, the soil becomes so compacted, it prevents new growth entirely.

Goats, though smaller than the cattle or water buffalo, are equally destructive. When goats feed, they nip a plant down to the ground, often pulling it out by the roots, killing the plant in the process. A herd of goats foraging in this way can denude large areas of the pastureland, converting once-lush floodplains into broad bands of dirt and mud incapable of supporting any type of animal life.

The Poison of the Gold Rush

The floodplain is not the only part of the Amazon ecosystem to suffer from commercial development. Gold mining has also taken a terrible toll on fish stocks within the Amazon River and its major tributaries. Large-scale mining operations that use heavy dredges churn up sediment on the riverbeds. As they try to avoid the water clouded by this activity, some fish are prevented from migrating to their spawning grounds. According to Goulding, Smith,

The Amazing Floating Meadows

One of the many unique features of the floodplain is the floating meadow. These meadows, which have been measured up to one square mile, are large bogs made up a variety of thickly matted and intertwined vegetation such as clusters of grasses, broad-leafed floating plants such as giant lilies, and reeds. What makes these meadows so unusual is that none of the plants are rooted in the riverbed. All of them extend their roots into the water, from which they satisfy all their nutritional needs. One of the advantages of these meadows is that most of the aquatic plants that form them have constant exposure to sunlight as they float.

Floating meadows form along the banks of protected floodplains far from swift-moving water. As they slowly glide with the sluggish currents, they attract hundreds of species of insects, worms, and arachnids that prefer to lay their larvae on these meadows because of the nutrient-rich vegetation. The larvae in turn attract a variety of fish that feed on them around the edges of the meadows.

As the fish eat in the midst of these floating meadows, they lay their eggs or give birth to fry, which adds another dimension to their usefulness as nurseries for young fish. Capable of swimming deep within the vegetation, young fish are able to hide from predators while feeding on the insects and worms that often fall into the water.

and Mahar, mining the rivers now involves "the use of several thousand barges, some 20 helicopters, 750 small planes, and perhaps 10,000 boats or motorized canoes. In general, greater mechanization has led to increased pollution." [16]

Some fish manage to find their way to spawning grounds despite the disruptions, but the churning activity of the dredges is, unfortunately, only the first step in the gold mining process. The process of extracting the gold from the dredged-up sediment exacts an even heavier toll on fish. After the river sand and gravel is scooped up, large amounts of mercury are washed through the sediment to extract gold through a process called amalgamation. The mercury binds to the gold flakes, causing them to separate from sand and gravel. Once the gold and mercury is isolated, a hot flame is applied to these two bonded metals, causing the mercury to evaporate and leave the gold behind. Once the process has finished, the vaporized mercury condenses, and this, along with most of the mercury that did not bind with gold in the first place, is washed down the river.

When mercury enters the rivers, microorganisms absorb it in a biochemical process called methylation. The mercury then enters the food chain as the fish eat the microorganisms. The mercury kills many fish outright; each year, tons of dead contaminated fish wash up along the banks of the Amazon River and its tributaries. The mercury then moves up the food chain as animals that come across these dead fish eat them. They also become sick—and die—if they eat too much of the contaminated fish. Of particular concern to medical researchers is the fact that sometimes people catch and eat the contaminated fish as well, and may suffer devastating neurological damage and even death.

Environmental Consequences of Dams

Other forms of exploitation of the Amazon cause more subtle but no less devastating harm. The hydroelectric dams built on some of the Amazon's tributaries have been a boon to businesses, villages, and cities but a bane to the environment.

Although the dams have dramatically increased the supply of cheap electricity, they have inflicted considerable damage on the Amazon Basin's ecology.

The most visible environmental damage is the permanent flooding of lowland forests. For example, the Balbina dam reservoir on the Rio Uatumã flooded an area of 583,000 acres of forest, including an estimated 145,000 acres of timber. In addition to the trees, all animals living in this area were either drowned or driven from their habitat.

Less visible but just as destructive in terms of long-term impact is an effect agronomists call siltation, the accumulation of silt in reservoirs. Before the building of the dams, the rivers carried silt, which is a natural fertilized soil made up of minerals and organic material, along with the water. During the great annual flood when the Amazon overflows, the water carried thousands of tons of silt to the floodplain, where it nourished the forests. Where the rivers are dammed, the silt is trapped at the bottom of the many reservoirs, so it no longer reaches the floodplain's forests.

Of all the effects of the dams, however, biologists consider their impact on migratory species of fish to be the worst. The many dams that now span various tributaries within the Amazon River network create imposing obstacles to the migration of fish. Besides having their migration routes blocked, fish trying to migrate back downriver are often sucked into the dams' turbines and pulverized by the spinning blades.

Overfishing

In addition to the damage done to fish stocks by the disruption of migration routes, overfishing is another major threat to many species. During the decades of the 1960s and '70s, as commercial fishing fleets grew and sailed the Amazon River and its many tributaries, the bounty of the rivers seemed limitless. Ships returned to the major ports and unloaded tons of fish from their brimming holds. So many fish were pulled from the rivers during that time that they sold for less than chicken, which historically had been the cheapest form of animal protein in the region.

The Plight of the Cardinal Tetra

Large commercial fish of the Amazon River are not the only ones prized by fishermen. Some of the smallest fish suffer along with the largest from excessive fishing to meet the demands of tropical-fish hobbyists throughout the world. The Amazon River Basin is one of the major sources for ornamental fish that eventually end up in home aquariums.

Of all the beautiful ornamental fish found in the Amazon, the one most prized is the cardinal tetra, *Paracheirodon axelrodi*. Like many of its related subspecies, the cardinal tetra is about two inches long, and is recognizable by a vivid cardinal red stripe running the length of its body. Part of this fish's popularity is that they always school together. So, enthusiasts like to have a large number of them in an aquarium for a dramatic presentation.

The exporting of these tiny fish is based on an unfortunate economic system. The fishermen who capture these fish in nets are poor and desperately in need of money. They are paid $1 per thousand fish. The fish are then packaged and flown out of the airport at Manaus to major cities throughout the world. By the time the cardinal tetras reach tropical-fish shops, their price has ballooned to $10 per fish, an increase of 10,000 percent.

Although there are millions of these small fish in the rivers, their numbers are declining because of overfishing, coupled with loss of breeding grounds. Breeding in captivity has been attempted, but thus far it has proven to be largely unsuccessful because of the impossibility of re-creating the fish's natural habitat.

The beautiful cardinal tetra is prized by tropical fish enthusiasts.

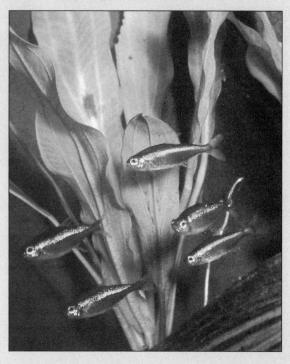

The day's catch is unloaded on the wharf to be transported to a local market in Brazil. Overfishing in the Amazon has resulted in greatly reduced catches, however.

After four decades of large-scale fishing, however, the illusion of limitless fish has been destroyed. Studies performed by governments within the Amazon Basin portray a steady decline of commercial fish populations since the 1970s. According to biologists, overfishing, along with deforestation, is a principal cause of the decline. Statistics tell the story. The piramutaba catfish, for example, dropped from an export peak value of $13 million to a low of $3 million in the mid-1990s because of declining stocks. Various species of characin, a common species related to carp and catfish, have faced similar declines. In 1980, this family of fish accounted for approximately 46.5 million pounds, but by 1990 this number decreased to only 29.5 million pounds.

The tambaqui has suffered a similar fate. This fish was so prevalent during the late nineteenth century that José Veríssimo, an observer of the Amazon River at the time, reported, "The tambaqui is captured in such large quantities for the Manaus market that the unsold excess was fed to prisoners." [17] In 1980, thirty-five hundred tons were taken, but today the catch is so small that this sought-after fish only appears on the menus of the most expensive restaurants. According to Roy G. Belville at the University of Michigan, "The tambaqui, like many forest fishes of the Amazon, is currently being threatened. . . . Excessive commercial fishing, which favors big fish like tambaqui, is taking its toll on populations. The fish has nearly been fished out of the waters around Manaus, Brazil, where the Rio Negro and Amazon converge." [18]

As the mature commercial fish decline in numbers, fishermen turn to the juvenile fish that inhabit the small tributaries and the floodplain. The young remain here until they reach adult size because they are not yet strong enough to survive the fast currents of the main rivers or to escape the predators found there. Fishing for juveniles of any species is alarming to biologists because the practice is certain to cause populations to diminish even further. When juveniles are taken, they never mature into large fish, which have greater value to the fishing industry. Consequently, larger numbers of the juvenile fish must be caught to compensate for the lack of larger adult fish. A cycle of ever-declining catches ensues. Unless this cycle can be interrupted, biologists fear that some species will eventually become endangered and possibly extinct.

Victims of Fortune

Although fish have suffered more than any other animal along the Amazon River, they are not the only victims of the recent development in the region. The chase to profit

Loss of Biological Balance

One of the secondary effects of the commercialization of the Amazon River and its floodplain has been a loss of many of the biological balances necessary to sustain healthy wildlife stocks. One of the causes of imbalances is the depletion of some types of animal species but not others. When this type of imbalance is multiplied many times within a specialized habitat such as the Amazon River, all species can suffer. An excellent example is the boto dolphin.

The boto is one of the largest inhabitants of the river and possesses one of the largest appetites. Mature adults weighing three hundred pounds are capable of consuming thirty pounds of fish each day. This enormous daily intake, more than twenty times more food than equally large fish eat, is due to their exceptionally high metabolism. As a predator of fish, the boto is only one of many fish-eating species in the river, and it is surpassed in daily take only by commercial fishing boats. Although commercial fishing boats take far more fish than the boto, the problem of balance is that the boto has no predators, not even commercial fishermen.

Whenever a habitat has a major predator that has no natural enemies, many of the smaller species begin to disappear. As the boto eat and multiply without the threat of any predators, their numbers increase while the fish they depend on decrease. If this imbalance is not rectified, the small fish will continue to disappear until there are so few that the larger predators begin to die of starvation and commercial fishermen go out of business.

The survival of the boto is threatened by disruption of the ecological balance of the Amazon.

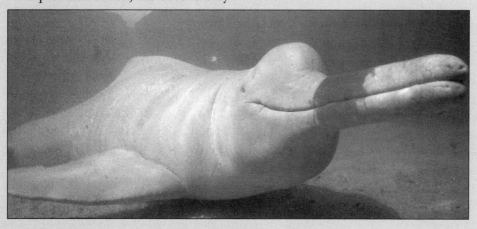

from gold, fish, lumber, cattle, electricity, and dozens of other natural resources along the river and its floodplain has collided with the interests of many indigenous peoples. In an area as large as the Amazon Basin, many small primitive tribes living miles from the nearest roads or towns and concealed by thick jungle foliage are largely forgotten, left to watch the advance of civilization.

Anthropologists say that some tribes still exist in remote regions that are unknown by government officials and unmapped by modern cartographers. Without any form of political recognition or representation, some of these tribes have suffered terribly at the hands of those hoping to profit from the exploitation of the resources of the Amazon River and its floodplain.

In 1980, for example, tribes such as the Kayapó and Xavante pressed for recognition and protection against gold prospectors who were invading their forests and polluting their rivers with deadly mercury. Chiefs were chosen by these small tribes to meet with conservation groups and anthropologists to assist them in reclaiming their lands and preserving their way of life. Unfortunately, no progress could be made because, although these tribes have existed in the Amazon River floodplain for hundreds of years, none possesses legal documents proving their ownership of the lands.

Government indifference toward indigenous tribes was illustrated in the mid-1980s when the Brazilian government advocated the sale of vast stretches of undeveloped land to poor itinerant Brazilians. The government advertised the land with the slogan "The land without people for the people without land." [19] What this catchy slogan obscured was the fact that the land did have people. Several small indigenous Indian tribes occupied the land at that time and had done so for hundreds of years. Yet, when the government sold the land, the buyers, with the assistance of the Brazilian government, forced the tribes from their home.

Collisions between modern and ancient ways of life have not favored the ancient ways. It is common for large corporations to purchase tracts of land from the government, unaware that tribes have lived there for generations and that they claim rights to the land based on tribal tradition. Regardless of their claims to the land, some tribes have been pushed aside and decimated by diseases spread by newcomers; some have even been killed by men hired to eliminate obstinate tribesmen who stand in the way of corporations bent on extracting natural resources.

Shelton Davis, director of the Anthropology Resource Center at Harvard University, compared the present Indian situation in Brazil to the experience of Native Americans at the hands of white settlers in the nineteenth century. He notes in his book *Victims of the Miracle* that just as the American Indians were once exterminated and chased from their traditional lands, the same outcome probably awaits the Brazilian Indians:

> It is clear that the Brazilian government is attempting to institutionalize a type of Indian policy similar to that practiced in the United States. . . . Without a major change in policy, and given the vast amount of economic activity now taking place in the Amazon Basin, one can only predict that the same fate awaits the remaining Indian tribes of Brazil. [20]

In spite of the destruction that unregulated development has wrought in the Amazon Basin, there is hope that the ecological harm is not irreversible. Scientists, government officials, and local residents have begun taking steps to end the most destructive activities and to find ways that humans can live in the region as part of a stable diverse ecosystem.

5
·········

Preserving the
Treasures of the River

Caring for the Amazon River and its floodplain so they can serve future generations requires addressing the political, economic, and social needs of those who depend on the river without placing further strain on it. To achieve these objectives, local and international agencies are now focusing on long-term solutions to the problems stemming from the commercial abuses of the past fifty years that have degraded the river's waters and wildlife.

Hope for the Amazon also rests on repairing the damage that has already been inflicted on the river. This task, which is recognized as essential by most of the scientific community, is now acknowledged as necessary by the Amazon Basin governments as well. Together, the scientists and policy makers are defining a plan to rectify the damage to the environment and to minimize further problems.

Highest on the list of priorities for healing the Amazon River has been helping save the fish populations from any further degradation. To accomplish this objective, those concerned sought new techniques to save the fish as well as to protect the commercial fishing industry.

Saving the Fish Through Aquaculture

Fishermen along the Amazon River as well as various government agencies recognize the need to protect fish stocks while at the same time protecting the jobs of fishermen. Both parties believe that aquaculture, the commercial farming of fish, may be the solution to this delicate balance of nature and commerce. Although aquaculture is not new, modern techniques show promise in restoring an industry that died out in the Amazon Basin thousands of years ago.

The fish of greatest interest to aquaculturists is the tambaqui. The National Institute of Amazonian Research, in cooperation with the Amazon Rivers Program of the Rainforest Alliance, has funded a project to farm tambaqui. Farming this or any other species involves containing the fish to protect them from the wilds of the river. This is generally accomplished either by fencing off a portion of a river with flexible netting to keep desired fish inside and preda-

Aquaculturalists hope to save the declining Amazon fish population by farming species such as the tambaqui (pictured).

tors out, or by constructing large earthen ponds a short distance from the river. When mature breeding fish lay their eggs or the fry hatch, the young are separated from the parents and fed highly nutritious foods to stimulate rapid growth. When they eventually reach market size, they are harvested.

The principal advantage of aquaculture is the ability to bring fish to market faster than when they are grown in the wilds of the rivers. Protected from predators yet fed with highly nutritious foods, the farmed fish grow quickly and in great abundance. The secondary advantage of fish farms is that the harvest does not require expensive boats or fishing gear. For example, with pond aquaculture, the ponds are simply drained and the fish scooped up.

When aquaculture is properly practiced, the sale of the farmed fish reduces pressure on wild fish populations, allowing gradual rebuilding of river fish stocks. The eventual hope among biologists and fishermen is to use aquaculture to assist in the repopulating of the rivers to keep the fishing industry alive and profitable. If this is possible, both fishermen and fish farmers will benefit.

Although fish farming is the primary focus in the Amazon Basin, shrimp farming is also increasing as a result of the growth in world demand. According to Jorge de la Rocha of the United Nations Food and Agriculture Organization's Regional Office for Latin America and the Caribbean, "Brazil is the 'sleeping giant' of South American fisheries."[21] La Rocha estimates that about seventy-five thousand acres are expected to be set aside for shrimp farming by 2003, when production is projected to reach nine thousand tons.

Cleansing the River

Aquaculture will only succeed, however, if the waters of the Amazon are cleaned of toxic pollutants. The worst pollutant in the Amazon River is the highly toxic mercury that is used in refining gold. An estimated two grams of mercury are released into the river for each gram of gold recovered, which adds up to more than one hundred tons of mercury annually.

The global action plan of the United Nations Industrial Development Organization has identified the necessary steps for the introduction of cleaner gold mining technologies. A project has been developed to help the governments of the seven Amazon River countries that engage in gold mining to continue doing so without contaminating the

The Work of Limnologists

Limnologists are scientists who study the many characteristics of inland freshwater rivers and lakes. In particular, these scientists seek to understand the geographical, chemical, and biological attributes of freshwater bodies in order to determine their ability to support wildlife, the water quality, and solutions to pollution problems.

One of the most prestigious institutes studying the Amazon River and its floodplain is the Max Planck Institute for Limnology. This German institute deals with the research of inland waters and their surrounding land in several areas of interest—in particular, evolutional and physiological backgrounds and interactions of organisms that lead to the development of communities.

The Max Planck Institute (whose website can be found at http://mpilim. mpilploen.mpg.de/mpiltalg.htm) is currently working to answer the following questions about the Amazon River floodplain:

- How does the flood pulse affect the physico-chemical conditions and the nutrient status in the soil and in the interstitial water?
- How does groundwater influence the nutrient status of floodplain lakes?
- How do herbaceous plants and trees of the floodplain forest respond to the oscillation between the terrestrial and the aquatic phases with respect to primary production and photosynthesis?
- How does the root system of trees respond to the oscillation between the terrestrial and the aquatic phases?
- How do terrestrial invertebrates manage to survive periodic flooding?
- Does the flood pulse induce peculiarities in the life cycle and behavior of terrestrial invertebrates that lead to genetic differentiation?
- How can the results be used for sustainable management and protection of floodplains?

environment with mercury. Although there is no practical alternative to the use of mercury itself, extraction can be conducted without mercury being released into the environment. The amalgamation process releases mercury in two ways: as a vapor and as a liquid. Therefore, chemists have developed two methods of capturing mercury before it can enter the river.

Mercury vapor released in the amalgamation process can be effectively captured before it escapes into the atmosphere by using enclosed cooking vessels called retorts. When heat is applied to separate the mercury from the gold, the vaporized mercury is trapped in these vessels and later safely removed. Retorts reduce atmospheric emissions of mercury by up to 99 percent.

The liquid mercury that is washed directly into the rivers can now be removed by a filtration process using activated carbon. The unused mercury that is mixed in with sand and gravel is filtered through layers of crushed activated carbon, which absorbs the mercury. The mercury-saturated carbon is later placed in a hot kiln, where the mercury vaporizes and is safely captured in a retort.

Addressing Hydroelectric Dam Problems

The hydroelectric dams built along the tributaries of the Amazon River have successfully provided energy for the Amazon Basin, but the costs to the fishing industry, displaced people, and the environment have been high. Civil and electrical engineers who specialize in designing these dams believe that there are alternatives to the dams that can provide needed electricity without harming the environment, the wildlife, or the local communities.

In Peru, an organization known as the Intermediate Technology Development Group (ITDG) and several banks have assisted small companies so that they can set up micro–hydroelectric power plants. Micro–hydroelectric sites are built on streams or beside tributaries where the cascade needed to spin the turbines that generate electricity is typically about thirty feet. Although this distance is not very great compared to large dams more than one hundred feet tall, a high volume of water can compensate for the low vertical drop. The greatest advantage of these micro–power plants is that they are usually built beside a river rather than blocking it altogether and only part of the river's water is diverted to the small dam.

The advantages of diverting only part of a river's water are substantial. Unlike large dams spanning an entire river, microdams do not prevent most fish from migrating up and down the river. Furthermore, the amount of land submerged by the reservoir is small, and these dams are never built where existing human populations will be displaced. Thus far, twenty-one new micro–hydroelectric plants have been constructed, benefiting approximately fifteen thousand people. According to Teodoro Sanchez, the ITDG energy program manager for Peru, "As our work in Peru shows these small scale schemes [micro–hydroelectric dams] are practical and can be efficiently managed by the communities themselves. The communities have been involved in the project from the start, have helped develop and shape the scheme to their needs, and can share this knowledge with others."[22]

A second form of micro–electrical generation is the use of solar power. Solar electrical power, or photovoltaic power, is electricity generated by silicon panels that convert sunlight to electricity. Although a relatively new form of power generation, it has wide application in sunny climates such as the Amazon Basin. In 2001, the Brazilian government announced the construction of a solar energy program that would provide solar panel farms, large banks of solar panels covering several acres, to supply power for electrical lights and small machinery in forty-five agricultural regions. The plan is to install 141 such systems by March 2002, with the installation of 687 by June 2002.

Electrical generation alternatives to the large dams currently contribute no more than 2 percent of the electrical needs in the Amazon Basin. Nonetheless, proponents of micro–power generators are optimistic that as these new technologies develop, fewer large dams will be needed.

Repairing Floodplain Soil Damage

A less technology-intensive solution exists for the problems caused by the ranches that now dot the Amazon floodplain. To counter the growing soil compaction problem, government agencies and private companies are supporting ranchers who are willing to replace cattle with vegetable farming. As the populations of all South American countries grow, the prices of some crops are rising, making them as profitable to produce as beef. The crops of greatest demand that bring high prices at the supermarkets are vegetables, especially tomatoes, lettuce, cucumber, bell peppers, and onions.

Replacing ranches with vegetable farms, such as this one, can help repair the damage from soil compaction caused by cattle.

The United Nations published a study on soil management and conservation for small farms in Brazil's floodplain, focusing on many issues, including the evaluation of the effects of cattle trampling on soil. The study found that in the most severe cases, compaction caused roots to grow too slowly or not deeply enough. Furthermore, when the floods arrive, the compacted soil prevents the water from being adequately absorbed.

To counter these problems, the study recommended the cultivation of vegetables and other commercial crops in place of grazing cattle. According to a United Nations study, after three years, the vegetable cultivation "led to lower production costs for crops and higher returns, combined with conservation and improvement of soil resources. As the compacted soils softened, the habitats began to return to the natural state before the large-scale herding of livestock."[23]

Returning to Traditional Farming

Many agronomists believe that the potential of the Amazon floodplain for growing crops is currently underutilized. One of the most important features of the Amazon River floodplain is its remarkably fertile soil. Rich in minerals and organic nutrients that are deposited each year by the annual flood, the black soil of the floodplain, which cattle and other livestock now trample, could be better utilized for crops. Some agronomists point out that cattle can survive and flourish on land where the soil is poor, because the grasses that cattle eat are hardy and are capable of thriving under difficult soil conditions. The same, however, cannot be said of high-yield crops. The great Amazon floodplain, agronomists say, could be developed into a major farming area. Steps have been taken recently to remove cattle from a few select floodplain locations and replace them with such products as fruits, vegetables, and nut-bearing trees.

Perhaps the best hope for the survival of the floodplain and its remaining forests is the growing recognition that trees are more valuable when left standing than when cut. Charles Peters and two colleagues at the Institute of Economic Botany at the New York Botanical Garden published the results of a three-year study that calculated the market value of dozens of exotic fruits that grow in the floodplains. The study, which appeared in the British journal *Nature*, asserts that, "over time selling these products could yield more than twice the income of either cattle ranching or lumbering."[24]

Small-Animal Ranching

Even some types of ranching could be practiced without damaging the floodplain further. The floodplain, which is underwater for at least half of the year, is an ideal environment for many small-animal ranches. Ducks, turkeys, chickens, and guinea fowl have been introduced in a few small areas because they are well suited to the semiaquatic geography of the floodplain. Agronomists believe that small-animal ranching is a viable alternative to cattle because such livestock will neither compact the soil nor trample the natural floodplain vegetation.

Not only does raising these different types of fowl not adversely affect the environment, but such ranches can be profitable. Fowl are able to thrive on the nuts, fruits, and seeds produced by indigenous trees. An added benefit of fowl is that raising them requires only a modest initial

Small-animal ranching is an environmentally sound alternative to cattle ranching.

investment. Fowl ranchers do not need to construct large complexes, truck in large quantities of building materials, or cut large roads through the floodplain forests as cattle ranchers do. Because they are physically small, fowl are also easy to transport. Placed in large wire cages, they are easily loaded on small boats and ferried to market.

Social Unrest

Sometimes disagreements between two opposing groups of people over the use of the Amazon River have escalated beyond reasonable discussion to violence. In the late 1980s, the Kayapó tribe forced the Brazilian government to abandon plans to build six huge dams on the Xingu River. The international uproar over environmental and human rights concerns was enough to persuade the World Bank to suspend financing for all dams in the Amazon Basin.

One of the most ardent and outspoken opponents of the dams on the Xingu was Ademir Alfeu Federicci, a Brazilian activist concerned with the environment and the people dependent on the environment. Federicci was opposed to the actions of the electric company, Eletronorte, charging that the company would make millions of dollars while ruining the river if it built hydroelectric dams. In 2001, Federicci was murdered. The Global Response website reported this story (called "Murder in the Amazon" at www.globalresponse.org.

The Belo Monte dam's most prominent critic was Ademir Alfeu Federicci, known to his neighbors as Dema. In addition to voicing environmental and human rights concerns, Dema denounced corruption among Xingu government officials who stand to gain from Eletronorte's compensation payments. Instead of opening serious democratic debate about the project, Eletronorte has intimidated opposition groups. In a letter to the president, Dema wrote, All public meetings against the dam have been filmed by police and intelligence forces. This is unacceptable in a debate over the future of the Amazon. At dawn on August 25 in his home, 36-year-old Dema was shot in the head in front of his wife and children. More than 3,000 people attended his funeral the next day. MDTX [an environmental regulatory commission] leaders have no confidence in local authorities who are unlikely to investigate the powerful interests behind the murder.

From the standpoint of environmentalists, a significant advantage to small-animal ranching is the preservation of the floating meadows that are crucial to the breeding of many indigenous fish species in the floodplain. In fact, fowl integrate themselves very well with these meadows. They are able to swim to the meadows, graze on insects and seeds, and even use them for nesting. Ranchers, however, must track the floating meadows to harvest clutches of eggs before they drift away. But even if they do, the meadows will continue to provide fish with safe spawning grounds and provide their fry with safe feeding grounds until they mature.

Government Protection of the River

The seven nations that control and supervise the Amazon River and its floodplain realize that they play a vital role in protecting this unique habitat. Most of these nations' governments continue to promote the exploitation of many of its natural resources, and they were initially slow to take effective measures to protect the environment. Today, however, they are beginning to recognize the importance of the habitat and have enacted many environmental laws and regulations aimed at preserving it.

Taking the lead are two Brazilian governmental agencies established to protect the Amazon River's fragile environment. The agency chartered to protect and promote the rational use of the floodplain is the Department for the Development of the Amazon. This agency regulates the use of the floodplain by conducting studies and overseeing commercial activities along the river. The other important agency, the Brazilian Institute of the Environment and Natural Resources, is an environmental institute that oversees the use and protection of most natural resources, such as timber, fish, commercial crops, and terrestrial wildlife.

One of the most acrimonious debates waged between environmentalists and the lumber industry before the Brazilian government was over the federal Forest Code. This code protects millions of Amazon Basin forests from logging. The government classified many river and flood-plain environments as permanent preservation areas, which means that logging in these delicate areas is banned. Forested areas away from riverbank areas are classified as legal reserve, which limits logging activities to a percentage of rural landholdings. Although the Forest Code now protects many trees, environmentalists believe that more acreage needs to be added, whereas logging companies argue that the code will destroy the economy in many rural areas.

The fishing industry, just like logging, has had curbs placed on its activities as well. The most crucial time of the year to ban or restrict fishing is during the spawning season. Various types of fishing bans have recently been effected to protect spawning fish in the floodplain, as well as migrating fish on the larger rivers. Governments have also recently applied size limits to fishing, which permit the capture of fish only above specified minimum lengths.

In addition to protecting the rivers and wildlife dependent on the rivers, Brazilian courts have begun enforcing laws governing the environment. In late May 2000, a federal judge suspended the bidding process for the construction of a canal because he found that the environmental impact report contained false information. In October of the same year, Judge Souza Prudente prohibited the loading and unloading of cargo ships at a newly constructed dock at the port in Barra because environmental permission for the new dock had never been granted. In rendering his decision, the judge recognized that "the environment is a universal right and . . . the right to life must prevail over individual economic interest." [25] And on December 6, 2001, a ban was placed on mahogany logging by the president of the Brazilian environmental agency, who stated, "Illegal mahogany logging in the Brazilian Amazon rainforest has been out of control for years, and has been responsible for the devastation of huge areas of pristine rainforest." [26]

Protecting the Amazon River and its floodplain while at the same time protecting the jobs in commercial industries

Satellites Study the Floodplains

Relatively little is known about the extent of flooding in the Amazon interior because of the difficulty of gaining access to it. In addition to obtaining a clear picture of Amazon flood patterns, scientists are interested in such things as determining the amount of water stored on floodplains during the wet season and the proportion of herbaceous versus woody vegetation. To learn more about these issues, researchers have turned to satellites for help.

Recently, the Japanese, with help from the Brazilians and Americans, have begun a new mapping effort using satellite remote sensing, which offers several advantages over earlier projects. Since mid-1995, synthetic aperture radar (SAR) aboard the Japanese Earth Resources Satellite-1 (JERS-1) has been collecting data from the Amazon Basin. The first data acquisitions of this project were of the Amazon rain forest during the low food season of 1995. It took sixty-two days to map the Amazon from coast to coast.

The longer radar wavelengths provided by the SAR are able to penetrate both clouds and forest. The return signal reveals the state of flooding beneath the forest canopy, allowing remote sensors to distinguish between woody and herbaceous plants. With the high-resolution data, scientists are able to determine the extent of flooding by comparing water extent for the dry and wet seasons. Knowledge of flood extent and land cover distributions will offer new insight into the Amazon's contribution to global methane emissions.

Floating meadows were also accurately mapped for the first time. High-resolution maps pinpointed these floating masses of vegetation. Researchers also determined that as water levels recede, the stems of the grasses begin to decay, causing a bubbling of methane gases. They also learned that the proportion of floating meadows increases toward the mouth of the Amazon.

All of this collected satellite data will also be valuable for evaluating the health of fisheries, which are essential to the physical and economic welfare of the people inhabiting the Amazon Basin.

for Amazonians is an important yet difficult balance to strike. If commercial development proceeds unchecked by environmental concerns, the inevitable destruction of this delicate habitat will fail the people living there. If, on the other hand, no commercial development is allowed, those living there will be forced to abandon their homes for jobs elsewhere. As Goulding, Smith, and Mahar write, "Any plan to conserve biodiversity and to sustainably manage natural resources must take into account the history, needs, and incentives that transformed the floodplain into what it is today and the forces that will drive future change." [27]

At present, the view taken by some scientists is that the recent surge in commercialization of the river and its floodplain has not yet yielded adequate statistics to indicate whether it is safe to increase commercialization or dangerous to do so. Other scientists, however, believe the risks of increasing commercialization in the floodplain, especially ranching, are too great and must be stopped. Not only have ranches caused the destruction of many forests and their soil, they have also caused the destruction of fragile ecosystems such as floating meadows and the fish they protect.

In spite of the present damage to the environment, some within the scientific community remain optimistic. These researchers believe that the relatively recent eruption of

After years of uncontrolled development of the Amazon Basin, governments, environmentalists, and scientists have formed coalitions to limit further exploitation of the river.

commercial interests along the Amazon River may be a gift in disguise for this habitat. Rather than creating an environmental catastrophe, there is hope that this habitat may create solutions to its own problems. According to Dr. Jeffrey Richey, a chemical oceanographer at the University of Washington, "So many of the world's big rivers have been manipulated by human activities that they bear no resemblance to a natural river anymore. . . . But it is not true of the Amazon, at least not yet, and that amounts to a big plus for science. We very much regard the Amazon as a big natural laboratory." [28]

After several decades of uncontrolled exploitation of the many gifts of the Amazon, governments, environmentalists, and scientists have formed coalitions to place controls on commercial ventures along the world's mightiest river. Although some hail this as an end to commercialization, many others realize that compromises must be made to serve the interests of everyone who depends on the generosity of this great river.

Notes

· · · · · · · ·

Introduction: One River for Two Seasons

1. Michael Goulding, Nigel J.H. Smith, and Dennis J. Mahar, *Floods of Fortune: Ecology and Economy Along the Amazon.* New York: Columbia University Press, 1995, p. 3.

Chapter 1: An Ocean of Water

2. Goulding, Smith, and Mahar, *Floods of Fortune,* p. 10.

Chapter 2: The Early Amazon

3. Clark L. Erickson, "An Artificial Landscape-Scale Fishery in the Bolivian Amazon," *Nature,* September 9, 2000, p. 190.
4. Erickson, "An Artificial Landscape-Scale Fishery in the Bolivian Amazon," p. 193.
5. Quoted in Robin Furneaux, *The Amazon: The Story of a Great River.* New York: G.P. Putnam's Sons, 1970, p. 34.
6. Erickson, "An Artificial Landscape-Scale Fishery in the Bolivian Amazon," p. 192.
7. Jean E. Jackson, *The Fish People: Linguistic Exogamy and Tukanoan Identity in Northwest Amazonia.* New York: Cambridge University Press, 1983, p. 45.
8. Philippe Descola, *The Spears of Twilight: Life and Death in the Amazon Jungle,* trans. Janet Lloyd. New York: New Press, 1996, p. 323.

Chapter 3: The Floods of Fortune

9. Quoted in Brendan Bernhard, *Pizarro, Orellana, and the Exploration of the Amazon.* New York: Chelsea House, 1991, p. 17.
10. Quoted in Bernhard, *Pizarro, Orellana, and the Exploration of the Amazon,* p. 19.
11. Quoted in Bernhard, *Pizarro, Orellana, and the Exploration of the Amazon,* p. 72.

12. Quoted in Helen and Frank Schreider, *Exploring the Amazon.* Washington, DC: National Geographic Society, 1970, p. 178.

Chapter 4: The Floods of Distress

13. Goulding, Smith, and Mahar, *Floods of Fortune,* pp. 1–2.
14. Goulding, Smith, and Mahar, *Floods of Fortune,* p. 45.
15. Quoted in Eugene Linden, "Playing with Fire Destruction of the Amazon Is One of the Great Tragedies of History," *Time,* September 18, 1989, p. 86.
16. Goulding, Smith, and Mahar, *Floods of Fortune,* p. 52.
17. Quoted in Goulding, Smith, and Mahar, *Floods of Fortune,* p. 97.
18. Roy G. Belville, *"Colossoma macropomum,"* University of Michigan. www.umich.edu.
19. Quoted in Sue Branford and Oriel Glock, *The Last Frontier: Fighting over Land in the Amazon.* Avon, England: Zed Books, 1985, p. 62.
20. Shelton H. Davis, *Victims of the Miracle.* London: Cambridge University Press, 1982, p. 107.

Chapter 5: Preserving the Treasures of the River

21. Quoted in Tom Wray, "Brazil's Big Plans," Industrial Shrimp Action Network. www.shrimpaction.com.
22. Teodoro Sanchez, "Planners and Builders Must Now Consider All Alternatives to Large Dams," Intermediate Technology Development Group. www.itdg.org.
23. Valdemar Hercilio de Freitas, *Soil Management and Conservation for Small Farms: Strategies and Methods of Introduction, Technologies, and Equipment.* Rome: Food and Agriculture Organization of the United Nations, Bulletin 77, 2000, p. 9.
24. Charles M. Peters, A. Gentry, and R. Mendelsohn, "Valuation of a Tropical Forest in Peruvian Amazonia," *Nature,* vol. 339, 1989, p. 657.
25. Quoted in Brazil Network, "Hidrovia/Waterway." www.brazil-network.org.

26. Quoted in Amanda Brown, "Greenpeace Welcomes 'Historic' Ban on Mahogany Logging," December 6, 2001. http://forests.org.
27. Goulding, Smith, and Mahar, *Floods of Fortune,* p. 165.
28. Jeffrey Richey, "The Amazon: A Big Natural Laboratory," Social, Behavioral, Economic Sciences. www.nsf.gov.

For Further Reading

Jacques Yves Cousteau and Mose Richards, *Jacques Cousteau's Amazon Journey.* New York: H.N. Abrams, 1984. This book describes Cousteau's trip up the Amazon from its mouth and his son Jean-Michel's expedition from its source at Mount Mismi in the Peruvian Andes. As with all Cousteau books, this one has many wonderful descriptions and color photographs of the Amazon River's wildlife.

Alan Greerbrant, *The Amazon: Past, Present, and Future.* Trans. Mark Paris. New York: Harry N. Abrams, 1992. A relatively brief history of the Amazon Basin with particular focus on the peoples living there. One of the strengths of the book is the copious use of art depicting the Indians, the river, and the wildlife of the forests.

Wolfgang J. Junk, *The Central Amazon Floodplain: Ecology of a Pulsing System.* New York: Springer-Verlag, 2001. This is perhaps the best technical discussion of the Amazon River floodplain. It is written by one of the foremost limnologists, who describes in detail the unique characteristics of this ecological region.

Candace Slater, *Entangled Edens: Visions of the Amazon.* Berkeley: University of California Press, 2002. This book traces the history of the Amazon, focusing on the influence of widely different groups of people from the conquistadors to corporate executives to subsistence farmers. The author takes the position that this environment and its dazzling wildlife cannot be saved without understanding those who live there.

Works Consulted

Books

Brendan Bernhard, *Pizarro, Orellana, and the Exploration of the Amazon*. New York: Chelsea House, 1991. This book tells the story of the sixteenth-century exploration of the Amazon by Spanish and Portuguese conquistadors. The book chronicles their passage upriver, tribes they encountered, and their hardships as they searched for the mythical city of El Dorado.

Sue Branford and Oriel Glock, *The Last Frontier: Fighting over Land in the Amazon*. Avon, England: Zed Books, 1985. This book traces the history of the Amazon from the original Indian populations to the region's opening to development. The book details the often violent conflicts that have occurred between native populations and powerful economic groups that threaten their existence.

Gaspar de Carvajal, *The Discovery of the Amazon According to the Account of Friar Gaspar de Carvajal and Other Documents*. Trans. Bertram T. Lee. New York: American Geographical Society, 1934. An account of Orellana's journey along the Amazon River written in 1542 by Gaspar de Carvajal. It is one of the very rare firsthand accounts of the expedition and provides an excellent source of what the conquistadors encountered.

Napoleon A. Chagnon, *Yanomanö: The Last Days of Eden*. New York: Harcourt Brace Jovanovich, 1992. Chagnon is an American anthropologist who lived among the Yanomanö tribesmen over a thirty-year period. He describes their culture, focusing on intratribal relationships as well as their relationships with other tribes, both friendly and belligerent.

Shelton H. Davis, *Victims of the Miracle*. London: Cambridge University Press, 1982. This book argues that the Brazilian government's economic policies during the 1970s caused an unacceptable amount of human suffering for the poor living in the Amazon Basin.

Philippe Descola, *The Spears of Twilight: Life and Death in the Amazon Jungle.* Trans. Janet Lloyd. New York: New Press, 1996. This work describes Descola's travels through the rain forest jungle in search of isolated tribes. He describes their lives in terms of their harmony with nature and their interactions with others, including the murders of their friends and fear of outsiders.

Valdemar Hercilio de Freitas, *Soil Management and Conservation for Small Farms: Strategies and Methods of Introduction, Technologies, and Equipment.* Rome: Food and Agriculture Organization of the United Nations, Bulletin 77, 2000. This publication is a detailed and technical work highlighting agricultural improvements in the Amazon Basin. In addition to the studies on soils and crops, recommendations are made regarding lightweight machinery and harvesting practices.

Robin Furneaux, *The Amazon: The Story of a Great River.* New York: G.P. Putnam's Sons, 1970. A general history of the Amazon River covering the early explorers, the wildlife of the basin, and the natural resources that attracted the early industry that eventually began to damage this tropical rain forest.

Karen Furnweger, *Amazon Rising: Seasons of the River.* Chicago: Shedd Aquarium Society, 2000. This is a short yet highly educational booklet that discusses the unique characteristics of the Amazon River floodplain. The booklet describes what makes this habitat unusual, its importance to the Amazon Basin, the wildlife, geology, and present environmental concerns.

Michael Goulding, *Amazon: The Flooded Forest.* New York: Sterling, 1990. This is an excellent nature book that investigates the Amazon and the bountiful wildlife it supports. Goulding discusses the river, the rain forest, and the array of plants and animals that make their home in and around the waters of the Amazon. Beautiful color photographs accompany the text.

Michael Goulding, Nigel J.H. Smith, and Dennis J. Mahar, *Floods of Fortune: Ecology and Economy Along the Amazon.* New York: Columbia University Press, 1995. This is the best book available on the Amazon River and its floodplain. It discusses the nature of the Amazonian rivers and floodplains and the economic and cultural events that have led to their drastic transformation. Most emphasis is placed on the Amazon River, but some attention is also paid to some of the tributaries. The book also contains excellent color photographs.

Caryl P. Haskins, *The Amazon: The Life History of a Mighty River*. Garden City, NY: Doubleday, Doran Company, 1943. This semitechnical book covers all aspects of the Amazon River, including its history, geography, geology, anthropology of the tribes, and the exotic display of wildlife.

Jean E. Jackson, *The Fish People: Linguistic Exogamy and Tukanoan Identity in Northwest Amazonia*. New York: Cambridge University Press, 1983. This work details the lives of several tribes living in the Amazon Basin, focusing on family and communal interactions.

Helen and Frank Schreider, *Exploring the Amazon*. Washington, DC: National Geographic Society, 1970. The lively narrative and beautiful pictures describe a trip taken by two anthropologists who navigate the Amazon River from Peru through Brazil. The book provides an excellent view of the river and its peoples prior to most large-scale commercialization.

Periodicals

Clark L. Erickson, "An Artificial Landscape-Scale Fishery in the Bolivian Amazon," *Nature*, September 9, 2000.

Eugene Linden, "Playing with Fire Destruction of the Amazon Is One of the Great Tragedies of History," *Time*, September 18, 1989.

Charles M. Peters, A. Gentry, and R. Mendelsohn, "Valuation of a Tropical Forest in Peruvian Amazonia," Nature, vol. 339, 1989.

Websites

Brazil Network (www.brazilnetwork.org). Brazil Network provides educational information on social, environmental, and cultural issues. This site also provides excellent photographs in stories about the Amazon River.

Forest Conservation Portal (www.forests.org). This website, maintained by Forests.org, Inc., contains thousands of articles about forests around the world. The site provides many links to other Internet resources dealing with forest conservation issues.

Global Response (www.globalresponse.org). Global Response reports environmental concerns around the world and encourages its readers to become actively involved in stopping the destruction of many endangered habitats.

Industrial Shrimp Action Network (www.shrimpaction.com). Industrial Shrimp Action Network was formed to support and encourage sustainable, responsible shrimp farming. Its website contains numerous examples of successful shrimp farming operations.

Intermediate Technology Development Group (www.itdg.org). ITDG is an international nongovernmental organization that specializes in helping people use technology in areas of acute poverty. The website provides information about the organization's work around the world.

Max Planck Institute (http://mpilim.mpil-ploen.mpg.de). This website outlines the institute's aims and methodologies in the Amazon River. It contains discussions of its current projects as well as a few diagrams that explain the importance of the relationship between the river and the floodplain.

National Geographic News (http://news.nationalgeographic.com) This website presents a variety of articles on the environment, science, and travel.

Social, Behavioral, Economic Sciences (www.nsf.gov.) This website, financed by the National Science Foundation, reports the research that promotes fundamental knowledge of human behavior and social and economic systems, organizations, and institutions.

University of Michigan (www.umich.edu). This site provides links to all activities and research carried out by faculty at the university.

Index

afterlife, 45–46

agriculture. *See* farming; fishing; ranching

amalgamation, 73

Amazon: Past, Present, and Future, The (Greerbrant), 38

Amazon River
boats used on, 42–44, 60–61
cleanup of, 83–85
confluence of, 18
geology of, 21
Pará, 22
rain forest of, 14
size of, 12–13, 21
source of, 16–17
see also early civilizations; ecology; explorers; farming; fish; floodplain; floods

Amazon River Basin
floodplain of, 10
geology of, 21
protected by Forest Code, 91–92
shrimp farming in, 83
solar power in, 86

Amazon Rivers Program of the Rainforest Alliance, 82–83

anaconda snakes, 26–27, 37–38

Andes Mountains, 21, 63

animals, 26–28
floodplain and, 23–24
frogs, 39–40
pygmy marmoset, 25
storytelling about, 45
see also individual animal names

Anthropology Resource Center, Harvard University, 80

aquaculture, 36–37, 82–83
see also fish; fishing

Atlantic Ocean, 20–22

Balbina dam reservoir, 74

balsa logs, 44

barbasco (poisonous plant), 35

bark canoes, 43

basin irrigation, 41–42

Belville, Roy G., 77

biodiversity, 14, 78, 94
see also ecology

"black soil," 41–42

blowguns, 39

boats
for commercial fishing, 60–61
rafts, 44
used by early civilizations, 42–44

boto dolphins, 27–28, 78

bows and arrows, 34, 35, 38

Brazil
energy used by, 62–63
fire in, 69
native population of, 79
protection of Amazon River in, 91
shrimp farming in, 83
social unrest in, 90

Tapajós, importance of, 19–20
Brazilian Highlands, 21, 63

caimans, 27, 37–38
canoes, 42–44
capybaras, 40
cardinal tetras, 75
Carvajal, Gaspar de, 40, 49–52
catfish, 61
characin, 76–77
cinnamon, 49–50
color, 22, 25
crustaceans, 62, 83

dams, 62–64, 73–74, 85–86
Davis, Shelton, 80
deforestation, 66–68, 76
Department of the Amazon, 91
Descola, Philippe, 45
detritus, 14, 18–19
dourada, 61
dugout canoes, 42–43

early civilizations, 32–33
  aquaculture by, 36–37
  basin irrigation by, 41–42
  fishing by, 33–36
  hunting by, 37–40
  spiritual life of, 44–46
  travel by, 42–44
ecology, 10
  biodiversity, 14, 78, 94
  damage from livestock and,
    70–72
  dams and, 73–74
  ecosystem, 9
  effect of gold rush, 72–73
  electricity and, 63–64

logging and, 57–59, 66, 91–92
native populations and, 79–80
ranching and, 68–70
river cleanup and, 83–85
see also animals; plants
economy, 93–94
  gold, 56
  logging and, 57–59
  ranching, 59–60
  rubber, 55
  spices, 48–50, 52–53
El Dorado, 47
electricity, 62–64, 73–74, 85–86
encontro das águas (meeting of
  the waters), 18
Erickson, Clark L., 36–37, 41
Europeans
  arrival of, 48–50
  rubber used by, 53
explorers, 47–48
  Gold Rush and, 55–57
  Orellana, 49–52
  Spanish and Portugese, 53

farming
  aquaculture, 82–83
  crops for, 88
  by early civilizations, 40
  soil management for, 87–88
fauna. See animals; fish
Federicci, Ademir Alfeu, 90
fire, 69
fish
  aquaculture, 36–37, 82–83
  cardinal tetras, 75
  characin, 76–77
  deforestation and, 66–68
  effects of dams on, 74

floating meadows and, 70, 72, 91, 93
habitats of, 25
juvenile, 77
migration of, 74
number of species of, 23
piramutaba catfish, 76
piranhas, 61
pirarucu, 61–62
spawning of, 92
tambaqui, 60, 77, 82–83
techniques to save, 81
fishing
  aquaculture, 36–37, 82–83
  commercial, 81
  by early civilizations, 33–36
  fisheries, 60–62
  overfishing, 74–77
  restrictions on, 92
floating meadows, 70, 72
  mapping of, 93
  small-animal ranching and, 91
floodplain, 22–24
  basin irrigation by early civiliza-
    tions, 41–42
  environmental effects on, 65–66
  hardwoods in, 58
  livestock and, 70–72
  regulated use of, 91
  for small-animal ranches, 89–91
  soil damage to, 71, 87–88
  studied by satellites, 93
  see also farming
floods, 8–11
  caused by dams, 74
  extent of, 23–24
  livestock and, 70–72
  patterns of, 93

studying, 84
  see also floodplain
flora. See plants
food
  from jungle, 40–41
  snakes as, 38
  see also aquaculture; fishing;
    hunting
Forest Code, 91–92
forests
  deforestation, 66–68
  logging of, 57–59
fowl, 89–90
freshwater, 20–22, 49
frogs, poisonous, 39–40

garimpeiros (gold prospectors),
  55–56
Global Response, 90
goats, 71–72
gods, 44
gold, 47–48
  amalgamation, 73
  cleaner techniques for, 84
  gold rush, 55–57, 72–73
Goulding, Michael, 10
  on aquatic vs. terrestrial habi-
    tats, 14
  on biodiversity, 94
  on Gold Rush, 72–73
  on logging, 66
  on slope of Amazon River, 21
government
  native populations and, 79
  protection of Amazon River by,
    91–95
  social unrest and, 90
"Green Hell," 14

Greerbrant, Alan, 38
Guiana Highlands, 21, 63

hardwood forests, 57–59, 66,
  92
  see also logging
Harvard University, 80
herbicides, 69
Hevea brasiliensis (rubber tree),
  53
Huaraco (Amazon headwaters),
  16–17
hunting, 37–40
hydroelectricity, 62–64, 73–74,
  85–86

insects, 31, 72
Intermediate Technology
  Development Group (ITDG),
  85–86
Itaipu River, 63

Jackson, Jean, 44
Japanese Earth Resources
  Satellite-1 (JERS-1), 93
Johnston, Andrew, 17

Kayapó tribe, 79, 90

LaFleur, Jim, 69
limnologists, 9, 84
livestock, 70, 72
  small-animal ranching vs., 89
  soil compaction by, 71, 87–88
logging, 57–59
  environmental impact of, 66
  Forest Code and, 91–92
lumber industry. See logging

Madeira, Rio, 16, 19
Mahar, Dennis, 10
  on aquatic vs. terrestrial habi-
    tats, 14
  on biodiversity, 94
  on gold rush, 72
  on logging, 66
mahogany, 92
Manaus, 55
maps, 14, 15, 49
Marajó Island, 33
Marañón River, 16
marombas (floating pens), 60
Max Planck Institute for
  Limnology, 84
mercury, 73, 83–85
methylation, 73
migration, of fish, 74
mosquitoes, 31

Napo River, 50–51
National Air and Space Museum,
  17
National Geographic Society, 17
National Institute of Amazonian
  Research, 82–83
native populations, 79
  *see also individual names of
    tribes*
Nature (magazine), 88
Negro, Rio, 16–19, 52
Nevado Mismi, 17

Opeko Dia (Milk River), 46
Orellana, Francisco de, 49–52

Pará (branch of Amazon River), 22
peccaries, 40

pele (ball of rubber), 54
Peru, 85–86
Peters, Charles, 88
photovoltaic power, 86
Pietowski, Andrew, 17
Pinzón, Vicente Yáñez, 48–49
piramutaba catfish, 61, 76
piranhas, 29, 61
pirarucu, 61–62
Pizarro, Gonzalo, 49, 52
plants
  as food, 41–42
  poisonous, 34–35
  spices, 48–50, 52–53
  water lilies, 28–30
  see also trees; *individual plant*
   names
poison
  from frogs, 39–40
  used for fishing, 34
poison-dart frogs, 39–40
Prudente, Souza, 92
pygmy marmoset, 25

rafts, 44
ranching, 59–60, 68–70, 89–91
Richey, Jeffrey, 95
rituals, of early civilizations, 44
roads, 68
Rocha, Jorge de la, 83
rubber, 53–55

salt water, 20–22, 49
Sanchez, Teodoro, 86
satellites, 93
schistosomiasis, 31
seeds, 14
seringueiro (tappers), 54

shrimp, 83
siltation, 74
Smith, Nigel, 10
  on aquatic vs. terrestrial habitats, 14
  on biodiversity, 94
  on gold rush, 72–73
  on logging, 66
Smithsonian Institution, 17
snow, 24
soil, 41–42, 70–71, 87–88
solar power, 86
spears, 37–38
Spears of Twilight: Life and
  Death in the Amazon Jungle,
  The (Descola), 45
spices, 48–50, 52–53
spiritual life, 44–46
stevedores, 48
storytelling, 45

tambaqui, 61, 77, 82–83
Tapajós, Rio, 16, 19–20
tapir, 37
tappers, 54
Tapuya tribe, 33
tetras, 75
tidal bores, 22
traps, 36–37
travel, by early civilizations,
  42–44
  see also boats
trees
  animal habitats of, 24–25
  for canoes, 42–44
  deforestation, 66–68
  hardwood, 57–59, 66, 92
  logging of, 57–59

mahogany, 92
tributaries, number of, 12–13
Tucuruí River, 63
Tukanoan tribe, 45
Tupí-Guaraní tribes, 33

Uatumã, Rio, 74
Ucayali River, 16
United Nations, 84, 87
University of Michigan, 77

várzea (floodplain), 22–24
  see also floodplain
Veríssimo, José, 77
Victims of the Miracle (Davis), 80

Waí Mahí (fish people), 34
water
  color of, 22, 25

confluence of, 18
level of, 23
quality of, 65
volume of, 13–16
  see also floodplain; floods
water buffalo, 70
water hyacinths, 30–31
water lilies, 28–30
weapons
  blowguns, 39
  bows and arrows, 34, 35, 38
  poison, 34, 39–40
  spears, 37–38
  weirs, 36–37

Xavante tribe, 79
Xingu, Rio, 16, 20

Yanomami tribe, 43

Picture Credits

• • • • • • • • • • • • • • • • • •

About the Author

James Barter is the author of more than a dozen nonfiction books for middle school students. He received his undergraduate degree in history and classics at the University of California Berkeley followed by graduate studies in ancient history and archaeology at the University of Pennsylvania. Mr. Barter has taught history as well as Latin and Greek.

A Fulbright scholar at the American Academy in Rome, Mr. Barter worked on archaeological sites in and around the city as well as on sites in the Naples area. Mr. Barter also has worked and traveled extensively in Greece.

Mr. Barter currently lives in Rancho Santa Fe, California, with his seventeen-year-old daughter, Kalista.